The Ecology Equation

Balancing Human Needs with Environmental Health

Rita Corbyn

The presentation of the information is without contract or any type of guarantee assurance. The trademarks that are used are without any consent, and the publication of the trademark is without permission or backing by the trademark owner. All trademarks and brands within this book are for clarifying purposes only and are the owned by the owners themselves, not affiliated with this document.

Table of Contents

Chapter 1

Introduction to Ecology and Human Impact

Understanding Ecology The Basics

Ecology, at its core, is the study of interactions between living organisms and their environment. It encompasses the intricate web of relationships that sustain life on Earth, from the smallest microorganisms to the largest mammals. Understanding these interactions is crucial for grasping the delicate balance that maintains the health of our planet. The basics of ecology provide a foundation for recognizing the profound impact humans have on natural systems and the importance of preserving ecological balance.

The concept of ecology can be traced back to the Greek word "oikos," meaning "house" or "dwelling." This etymology reflects the idea that all living organisms share a common home—the Earth—and are interconnected in a complex network of relationships. These relationships are governed by various ecological principles, such as energy flow, nutrient cycling, and population dynamics. Energy flow refers to the transfer of energy through an ecosystem, beginning with the capture of solar energy by plants through photosynthesis. This energy is then passed on to herbivores, carnivores, and decomposers, creating a food chain that sustains life.

Nutrient cycling, on the other hand, involves the movement of essential elements like carbon, nitrogen, and phosphorus through the environment. These nutrients are recycled through processes such as decomposition, respiration, and photosynthesis, ensuring their availability for future generations of organisms. Population dynamics, another key principle, examines the factors that influence the size and growth of populations within an ecosystem. These factors include birth and death rates, immigration and emigration, and the availability of resources.

Ecology is not limited to the study of individual species or populations; it also encompasses the interactions between different species and their environment. These interactions can be classified into several types, including competition, predation, mutualism, and commensalism. Competition occurs when two or more species vie for the same resources, such as food or habitat. This can lead to the exclusion of one species or the adaptation of both species to reduce competition.

Predation, another form of interaction, involves one species, the predator, feeding on another species, the prey. This relationship can have significant effects on the population dynamics of both species, as well as the overall structure of the ecosystem. Mutualism, in contrast, is a cooperative relationship between two species that benefits both parties. An example of mutualism is the relationship between bees and flowering plants, where bees obtain nectar for food while pollinating the plants.

Commensalism is a type of interaction where one species benefits while the other is neither helped nor harmed. An example of commensalism is the relationship between barnacles and whales, where barnacles attach themselves to the whale's skin, gaining access to nutrient-rich waters without affecting the whale. influence on natural systems has become increasingly apparent in recent decades, as our activities have led to significant changes in ecosystems worldwide. Deforestation, pollution, and climate change are just a few examples of how human actions have disrupted ecological balance. Deforestation, for instance, results in the loss of habitat for countless species, leading to declines in biodiversity and the disruption of nutrient cycling and energy flow.

Pollution, whether in the form of air, water, or soil contamination, can have devastating effects on ecosystems. It can lead to the accumulation of harmful substances in the environment, affecting the health of both plants and animals. Climate change, driven by the release of greenhouse gases from human activities, is causing shifts in temperature and precipitation patterns, altering the distribution and behavior of species.

The importance of ecological balance cannot be overstated, as it is essential for maintaining the health and stability of our planet. Ecological balance refers to the equilibrium between living organisms and their environment, where resources are used sustainably, and populations are kept in check. This balance ensures the continued availability of ecosystem services, such as clean air and water, fertile soil, and pollination, which are vital for human survival.

Historical perspectives on human-environment interaction reveal that humans have long been aware of their impact on the natural world. Ancient civilizations, such as the Greeks and Romans, recognized the importance of maintaining ecological balance and implemented practices to conserve resources and protect the environment. However, the industrial revolution marked a turning point in human history, as technological advancements and population growth led to increased resource consumption and environmental degradation.

The urgency of addressing ecological challenges has never been greater, as the consequences of human actions are becoming increasingly apparent. The loss of biodiversity, the depletion of natural resources, and the impacts of climate change are just a few of the pressing issues that demand immediate attention. To address these challenges, it is essential to adopt a holistic approach that considers the interconnectedness of all living organisms and their environment.

This approach involves recognizing the value of ecosystem services and incorporating them into decision-making processes. It also requires the development and implementation of sustainable practices that minimize environmental impact and promote ecological balance. Education and awareness are crucial components of this effort, as they empower individuals and communities to make informed choices and take action to protect the environment.

Human Influence on Natural Systems

Human activities have left an indelible mark on the natural systems of our planet, reshaping landscapes, altering ecosystems, and impacting biodiversity in profound ways. The influence of humanity on the environment is a complex tapestry woven from the threads of industrialization, urbanization, agriculture, and technological advancement. As we navigate the Anthropocene, the current geological age characterized by significant human impact on Earth's geology and ecosystems, it becomes imperative to understand the extent and nature of our influence on natural systems.

The dawn of agriculture marked the beginning of humanity's significant impact on the environment. As early humans transitioned from nomadic lifestyles to settled farming communities, they began to clear forests and modify landscapes to cultivate crops and raise livestock. This shift not only altered the physical environment but also set the stage for the development of complex societies. Over time, agricultural practices have evolved, leading to increased food production but also contributing to soil degradation, deforestation, and loss of biodiversity.

The industrial revolution, a pivotal moment in human history, further accelerated our influence on natural systems. The advent of machinery and the rise of factories transformed economies and societies, driving unprecedented levels of resource extraction and consumption. Fossil fuels became the lifeblood of industrialization, powering machines and transportation but also releasing vast amounts of greenhouse gases into the atmosphere. This marked the beginning of significant anthropogenic climate change, as the accumulation of carbon dioxide and other greenhouse gases began to alter global climate patterns.

Urbanization, another hallmark of human influence, has reshaped natural landscapes and ecosystems. As populations have grown and cities have expanded, vast areas of land have been converted from natural habitats to urban environments. This transformation has led to habitat fragmentation, loss of biodiversity, and increased pollution. Urban areas, with their high concentrations of people and infrastructure, also contribute to the urban heat island effect, where temperatures in cities are significantly higher than in surrounding rural areas due to human activities and altered land surfaces.

The extraction and consumption of natural resources have also played a significant role in shaping natural systems. Mining, logging, and fishing have provided essential materials and food for human societies but have often been conducted unsustainably, leading to habitat destruction, overexploitation of species, and pollution. The demand for resources has driven the expansion of human activities into previously untouched areas, further encroaching on natural habitats and threatening biodiversity.

Pollution, a byproduct of many human activities, has far-reaching effects on natural systems. Air pollution, resulting from the burning of fossil fuels and industrial processes, contributes to respiratory illnesses in humans and animals and can lead to acid rain, which harms ecosystems. Water pollution, caused by agricultural runoff, industrial discharges, and improper waste disposal, contaminates freshwater and marine environments, affecting aquatic life and human health. Soil pollution, often a result of pesticide use and industrial waste, degrades land quality and reduces agricultural productivity.

Climate change, driven by human activities, is perhaps the most pressing environmental challenge of our time. The increase in greenhouse gas emissions has led to rising global temperatures, melting ice caps, and shifting weather patterns. These changes have profound implications for natural systems, affecting species distribution, migration patterns, and ecosystem dynamics. Coral reefs, for example, are experiencing widespread bleaching due to rising sea temperatures, threatening the diverse marine life that depends on them.

Despite the significant impact of human activities on natural systems, there is hope for a more sustainable future. Efforts to mitigate and adapt to environmental challenges are gaining momentum, driven by a growing awareness of the need to balance human needs with ecological health. Sustainable practices, such as renewable energy adoption, conservation agriculture, and green urban planning, offer pathways to reduce our environmental footprint and promote ecological resilience.

Renewable energy technologies, such as solar, wind, and hydropower, provide alternatives to fossil fuels, reducing greenhouse gas emissions and air pollution. These technologies harness natural energy sources, offering a cleaner and more sustainable way to power human activities. The transition to renewable energy is a critical step in addressing climate change and reducing our impact on natural systems.

Conservation agriculture, which emphasizes soil health, biodiversity, and sustainable resource use, offers a way to produce food while minimizing environmental impact. Practices such as crop rotation, cover cropping, and reduced tillage help maintain soil fertility, reduce erosion, and enhance biodiversity. By adopting these practices, farmers can contribute to ecological balance while ensuring food security.

Green urban planning and architecture focus on creating sustainable and resilient cities that minimize environmental impact and enhance quality of life. Strategies such as green roofs, urban forests, and sustainable transportation systems help reduce pollution, mitigate the urban heat island effect, and promote biodiversity. By reimagining urban spaces, we can create environments that support both human and ecological well-being.

The role of policy and international agreements in addressing human influence on natural systems cannot be overstated. Initiatives such as the Paris Agreement aim to unite countries in the fight against climate change, setting targets for reducing greenhouse gas emissions and promoting sustainable development. National and local policies that support conservation, renewable energy, and sustainable resource management are essential for driving meaningful change.

Education and awareness are also crucial components of efforts to mitigate human impact on natural systems. By fostering a deeper understanding of ecological principles and the consequences of our actions, individuals and communities can make informed choices that support sustainability. Grassroots movements and environmental activism play a vital role in advocating for change and holding governments and corporations accountable for their environmental impact.

The Importance of Ecological Balance

Ecological balance is the harmonious relationship between living organisms and their environment, a delicate equilibrium that sustains life on Earth. This balance is essential for the health and stability of ecosystems, which provide vital services such as clean air and water, fertile soil, and pollination. The importance of maintaining ecological balance cannot be overstated, as it underpins the well-being of all living organisms, including humans.

The concept of ecological balance is rooted in the idea that ecosystems are dynamic systems, constantly changing and adapting to internal and external influences. These influences can include natural events, such as fires, floods, and storms, as well as human activities, such as deforestation, pollution, and urbanization. While ecosystems have a remarkable capacity to recover from disturbances, their resilience is not limitless. When the balance is disrupted beyond a certain threshold, ecosystems can experience irreversible changes, leading to the loss of biodiversity and the degradation of ecosystem services.

Biodiversity, the variety of life on Earth, plays a crucial role in maintaining ecological balance. Each species within an ecosystem has a specific function, contributing to processes such as nutrient cycling, energy flow, and population regulation. The loss of even a single species can have cascading effects, disrupting these processes and weakening the resilience of the ecosystem. For example, the decline of pollinator populations, such as bees and butterflies, can lead to reduced plant reproduction and lower crop yields, affecting food security and agricultural productivity.

The interdependence of species within an ecosystem is exemplified by the concept of keystone species. These are species that have a disproportionately large impact on their environment relative to their abundance. The removal of a keystone species can lead to significant changes in the structure and function of an ecosystem. For instance, the reintroduction of wolves to Yellowstone National Park in the United States has demonstrated the profound influence of keystone species. Wolves, as apex predators, help regulate the populations of herbivores such as elk, which in turn affects vegetation growth and the overall health of the ecosystem. activities have increasingly disrupted ecological balance, leading to a range of environmental challenges. Deforestation, driven by agriculture, logging, and urban expansion, results in habitat loss and fragmentation, threatening biodiversity and altering ecosystem dynamics. Pollution, whether from industrial emissions, agricultural runoff, or plastic waste, contaminates air, water, and soil, affecting the health of both ecosystems and human populations. Climate change, driven by the accumulation of greenhouse gases in the atmosphere, is causing shifts in temperature and precipitation patterns, affecting species distribution and ecosystem resilience.

The consequences of ecological imbalance are far-reaching and can have significant implications for human societies. The degradation of ecosystem services, such as clean water, fertile soil, and pollination, can lead to food and water scarcity, increased vulnerability to natural disasters, and economic losses. The loss of biodiversity can also reduce the availability of genetic resources, which are essential for developing new crops, medicines, and other products.

Addressing the challenges of ecological imbalance requires a multifaceted approach that considers the interconnectedness of all living organisms and their environment. Conservation efforts, such as the establishment of protected areas and the restoration of degraded habitats, play a vital role in preserving biodiversity and maintaining ecological balance. These efforts can help safeguard critical ecosystems, such as rainforests, wetlands, and coral reefs, which provide essential services and support a wide range of species.

Sustainable resource management is another key component of maintaining ecological balance. This involves adopting practices that minimize environmental impact and promote the sustainable use of natural resources. For example, sustainable forestry practices, such as selective logging and reforestation, can help maintain forest health and biodiversity while providing timber and other forest products. Sustainable agriculture practices, such as crop rotation, agroforestry, and integrated pest management, can enhance soil fertility, reduce chemical inputs, and support biodiversity.

The role of policy and governance in promoting ecological balance cannot be overlooked. National and international policies that support conservation, sustainable resource management, and climate change mitigation are essential for driving meaningful change. Initiatives such as the Convention on Biological Diversity and the Paris Agreement aim to unite countries in the effort to protect biodiversity and address climate change, setting targets and providing frameworks for action.

Education and awareness are also crucial components of efforts to maintain ecological balance. By fostering a deeper understanding of ecological principles and the consequences of human actions, individuals and communities can make informed choices that support sustainability. Environmental education programs, community-based conservation initiatives, and public awareness campaigns can empower people to take action and advocate for change.

Historical Perspectives on Human-Environment Interaction

The relationship between humans and the environment is as old as humanity itself, a dynamic interplay that has evolved over millennia. From the earliest hunter-gatherer societies to the complex industrial civilizations of today, humans have continuously interacted with their surroundings, shaping and being shaped by the natural world. Understanding the historical perspectives on human-environment interaction provides valuable insights into how past societies have managed resources, adapted to environmental changes, and sometimes faced the consequences of ecological imbalance.

In the earliest stages of human history, small bands of hunter-gatherers roamed the landscapes, relying on the bounty of nature for sustenance. These societies had a profound understanding of their environment, developed through generations of observation and experience. They knew the seasonal patterns of plants and animals, the locations of water sources, and the dangers posed by predators and natural disasters. Their impact on the environment was relatively minimal, as their nomadic lifestyle allowed ecosystems to recover and regenerate.

The advent of agriculture marked a significant turning point in human-environment interaction. As humans began to domesticate plants and animals, they settled in permanent communities, leading to the development of complex societies. Agriculture allowed for the production of surplus food, supporting larger populations and the growth of cities. However, it also required the modification of landscapes, as forests were cleared, and wetlands drained to create arable land. This transformation had profound ecological consequences, altering habitats and affecting biodiversity.

Ancient civilizations, such as those in Mesopotamia, Egypt, and the Indus Valley, developed sophisticated systems of irrigation and land management to support agriculture. These innovations allowed them to thrive in challenging environments, but they also highlighted the delicate balance between human needs and environmental health. The collapse of some ancient societies, such as the Maya and the Ancestral Puebloans, has been attributed in part to environmental factors, including deforestation, soil degradation, and water scarcity, exacerbated by human activities.

The industrial revolution, beginning in the late 18th century, marked another pivotal moment in human-environment interaction. The rise of factories and mechanized production transformed economies and societies, driving unprecedented levels of resource extraction and consumption. Fossil fuels became the primary energy source, powering machines and transportation but also contributing to air and water pollution. The industrial revolution brought about significant environmental changes, as landscapes were altered to accommodate factories, railways, and urban centers.

Urbanization, a hallmark of the industrial era, reshaped natural landscapes and ecosystems. As populations grew and cities expanded, vast areas of land were converted from natural habitats to urban environments. This transformation led to habitat fragmentation, loss of biodiversity, and increased pollution. Urban areas, with their high concentrations of people and infrastructure, also contributed to the urban heat island effect, where temperatures in cities are significantly higher than in surrounding rural areas due to human activities and altered land surfaces.

The 20th century witnessed a growing awareness of the environmental impact of human activities. The publication of Rachel Carson's "Silent Spring" in 1962 is often credited with sparking the modern environmental movement. Carson's work highlighted the dangers of pesticide use, particularly DDT, and its effects on wildlife and human health. Her book raised public awareness and led to increased scrutiny of industrial practices and their environmental consequences.

In response to growing environmental concerns, governments and organizations began to implement policies and initiatives aimed at protecting natural resources and promoting sustainability. The establishment of national parks and protected areas helped conserve critical ecosystems and biodiversity. International agreements, such as the Montreal Protocol and the Kyoto Protocol, sought to address global environmental challenges, including ozone depletion and climate change.

The late 20th and early 21st centuries have seen a shift towards recognizing the interconnectedness of human and environmental systems. The concept of sustainable development, popularized by the Brundtland Report in 1987, emphasizes the need to balance economic growth with environmental protection and social equity. This approach acknowledges that human well-being is inextricably linked to the health of the planet and that long-term prosperity requires the responsible management of natural resources.

Technological advancements have also played a role in shaping human-environment interaction. Innovations in renewable energy, such as solar and wind power, offer alternatives to fossil fuels, reducing greenhouse gas emissions and air pollution. Advances in agriculture, including precision farming and genetically modified crops, have the potential to increase food production while minimizing environmental impact. However, these technologies also raise ethical and ecological questions, highlighting the need for careful consideration and regulation.

As we look to the future, the lessons of history remind us of the importance of maintaining ecological balance and the consequences of failing to do so. The challenges of climate change, biodiversity loss, and resource depletion require a comprehensive and collaborative approach that considers the interconnectedness of all living organisms and their environment. By learning from the successes and failures of past societies, we can develop strategies to address these challenges and promote a sustainable future.

The Urgency of Addressing Ecological Challenges

The world stands at a critical juncture, facing a multitude of ecological challenges that threaten the very fabric of life on Earth. The urgency of addressing these challenges cannot be overstated, as the consequences of inaction are dire and far-reaching. From climate change and biodiversity loss to pollution and resource depletion, the environmental issues we face today are complex and interconnected, requiring immediate and concerted efforts to mitigate their impact and ensure a sustainable future.

Climate change, driven by the accumulation of greenhouse gases in the atmosphere, is perhaps the most pressing ecological challenge of our time. The burning of fossil fuels, deforestation, and industrial activities have led to a significant increase in carbon dioxide and other greenhouse gases, resulting in rising global temperatures. This warming has far-reaching effects, including melting ice caps, rising sea levels, and more frequent and severe weather events. The impacts of climate change are already being felt around the world, with vulnerable communities bearing the brunt of its effects.

The loss of biodiversity is another critical issue that demands urgent attention. Human activities, such as habitat destruction, pollution, and overexploitation of species, have led to a dramatic decline in biodiversity. This loss has profound implications for ecosystem health and resilience, as biodiversity plays a crucial role in maintaining ecological balance and providing essential services. The extinction of species not only diminishes the richness of life on Earth but also undermines the stability of ecosystems, making them more vulnerable to disturbances.

Pollution, in its many forms, poses a significant threat to both human and environmental health. Air pollution, resulting from the burning of fossil fuels and industrial emissions, contributes to respiratory illnesses and climate change. Water pollution, caused by agricultural runoff, industrial discharges, and plastic waste, contaminates freshwater and marine environments, affecting aquatic life and human health. Soil pollution, often a result of pesticide use and industrial waste, degrades land quality and reduces agricultural productivity. The pervasive nature of pollution underscores the need for comprehensive strategies to reduce emissions and manage waste effectively.

Resource depletion is another pressing ecological challenge, as the demand for natural resources continues to grow with increasing population and consumption. The extraction and consumption of resources, such as water, minerals, and fossil fuels, have led to habitat destruction, pollution, and the depletion of finite resources. The unsustainable use of resources not only threatens the environment but also poses significant risks to economic stability and human well-being. Addressing resource depletion requires a shift towards more sustainable practices, such as renewable energy adoption, circular economy models, and efficient resource management.

The interconnectedness of these ecological challenges highlights the need for a holistic approach to environmental management. Solutions must consider the complex interactions between human and natural systems, recognizing that actions in one area can have ripple effects across others. For example, efforts to reduce greenhouse gas emissions through renewable energy adoption can also help address air pollution and resource depletion. Similarly, conservation efforts that protect biodiversity can enhance ecosystem resilience and support climate change adaptation.

The role of policy and governance in addressing ecological challenges is crucial. National and international policies that support conservation, sustainable resource management, and climate change mitigation are essential for driving meaningful change. Initiatives such as the Paris Agreement aim to unite countries in the effort to reduce greenhouse gas emissions and promote sustainable development. However, the success of these initiatives depends on the commitment and cooperation of governments, businesses, and individuals.

Education and awareness are also vital components of efforts to address ecological challenges. By fostering a deeper understanding of environmental issues and the consequences of human actions, individuals and communities can make informed choices that support sustainability. Environmental education programs, community-based conservation initiatives, and public awareness campaigns can empower people to take action and advocate for change.

Technological innovation offers promising solutions to some of the most pressing ecological challenges. Advances in renewable energy, such as solar and wind power, provide alternatives to fossil fuels, reducing greenhouse gas emissions and air pollution. Innovations in agriculture, including precision farming and genetically modified crops, have the potential to increase food production while minimizing environmental impact. However, these technologies also raise ethical and ecological questions, highlighting the need for careful consideration and regulation.

The urgency of addressing ecological challenges is underscored by the potential consequences of inaction. The impacts of climate change, biodiversity loss, pollution, and resource depletion are already being felt around the world, with vulnerable communities disproportionately affected. Failure to address these issues could lead to further environmental degradation, economic instability, and social unrest. The stakes are high, but the opportunity for positive change is within reach.

Chapter 2

The Interconnected Web of Life

Ecosystems and Biodiversity A Primer

Ecosystems are the intricate webs of life that encompass all living organisms and their interactions with the physical environment. They range from the smallest pond to the vast expanse of the Amazon rainforest, each hosting a unique array of species and ecological processes. Biodiversity, the variety of life within these ecosystems, is a fundamental component that contributes to their resilience, productivity, and overall health. Understanding the basics of ecosystems and biodiversity is essential for appreciating the complexity of the natural world and the importance of preserving it.

At the heart of every ecosystem lies a delicate balance of biotic and abiotic components. Biotic components include all living organisms, such as plants, animals, fungi, and microorganisms, each playing a specific role in the ecosystem. Abiotic components encompass the non-living elements, such as sunlight, water, soil, and climate, which influence the conditions and resources available to the living organisms. The interactions between these components drive the flow of energy and nutrients, supporting the survival and reproduction of species.

Energy flow in ecosystems begins with the process of photosynthesis, where plants, algae, and some bacteria convert sunlight into chemical energy stored in organic compounds. These primary producers form the base of the food chain, providing energy and nutrients to herbivores, or primary consumers. In turn, herbivores are preyed upon by carnivores, or secondary consumers, which may themselves be consumed by higher-level predators. Decomposers, such as fungi and bacteria, play a crucial role in breaking down dead organic matter, recycling nutrients back into the ecosystem and maintaining soil fertility.

Biodiversity is a key factor in the stability and resilience of ecosystems. It encompasses the variety of species, genetic diversity within species, and the diversity of ecosystems themselves. High biodiversity enhances ecosystem productivity, as different species contribute to various ecological functions, such as pollination, seed dispersal, and nutrient cycling. This diversity also provides a buffer against environmental changes and disturbances, as ecosystems with a wide range of species are more likely to adapt and recover from stressors such as climate change, disease, and habitat loss.

The importance of biodiversity extends beyond ecological functions, as it also provides a wealth of resources and services that benefit human societies. Ecosystems supply essential goods, such as food, medicine, and raw materials, while also offering services like clean air and water, climate regulation, and recreational opportunities. The genetic diversity found in wild species is a valuable resource for developing new crops, pharmaceuticals, and other products, highlighting the need to conserve biodiversity for future generations.

Despite its importance, biodiversity is under threat from a range of human activities. Habitat destruction, driven by agriculture, urbanization, and infrastructure development, is the leading cause of biodiversity loss. As natural habitats are converted to human-dominated landscapes, species are displaced, and ecosystems are fragmented, reducing their ability to support diverse communities of organisms. Pollution, climate change, and the introduction of invasive species further exacerbate the pressures on biodiversity, leading to declines in species populations and, in some cases, extinction.

Conservation efforts are essential for protecting ecosystems and preserving biodiversity. These efforts can take many forms, from establishing protected areas and wildlife reserves to implementing sustainable land-use practices and restoring degraded habitats. Protected areas, such as national parks and nature reserves, provide safe havens for species and ecosystems, allowing them to thrive without the pressures of human activities. However, effective conservation requires more than just setting aside land; it also involves engaging local communities, promoting sustainable resource use, and addressing the underlying drivers of biodiversity loss.

Sustainable land-use practices, such as agroforestry, organic farming, and integrated pest management, can help maintain biodiversity while supporting agricultural productivity. These practices promote the conservation of natural habitats, reduce the use of harmful chemicals, and enhance the resilience of ecosystems to environmental changes. By adopting sustainable practices, farmers and land managers can contribute to the preservation of biodiversity while ensuring food security and economic stability.

Restoration of degraded habitats is another important aspect of conservation efforts. Restoration projects aim to rehabilitate ecosystems that have been damaged by human activities, such as deforestation, mining, or pollution. These projects often involve replanting native vegetation, removing invasive species, and restoring natural hydrological processes. Successful restoration can enhance biodiversity, improve ecosystem services, and provide opportunities for local communities to engage in conservation activities.

The role of policy and governance in biodiversity conservation is crucial. National and international policies that support conservation, sustainable resource management, and climate change mitigation are essential for driving meaningful change. Initiatives such as the Convention on Biological Diversity and the United Nations Sustainable Development Goals aim to unite countries in the effort to protect biodiversity and promote sustainable development. However, the success of these initiatives depends on the commitment and cooperation of governments, businesses, and individuals.

Education and awareness are also vital components of efforts to conserve ecosystems and biodiversity. By fostering a deeper understanding of ecological principles and the consequences of human actions, individuals and communities can make informed choices that support sustainability. Environmental education programs, community-based conservation initiatives, and public awareness campaigns can empower people to take action and advocate for change.

The Role of Keystone Species

In the intricate tapestry of ecosystems, certain species hold a disproportionately large influence over the structure and function of their environment. These are known as keystone species, a term that underscores their critical role in maintaining ecological balance. The concept of keystone species was first introduced by ecologist Robert Paine in the 1960s, who observed that the removal of a single species could lead to dramatic changes in an ecosystem. Understanding the role of keystone species is essential for appreciating the complexity of ecosystems and the importance of conserving biodiversity.

Keystone species can be found across various ecosystems, from the depths of the ocean to the heights of mountain ranges. They can be predators, prey, plants, or even microorganisms, each playing a unique role in their environment. What distinguishes a keystone species is not its abundance, but its impact. The removal or decline of a keystone species can trigger a cascade of changes, affecting the populations of other species and altering the ecosystem's structure and function.

One of the most well-known examples of a keystone species is the sea otter, which inhabits the coastal waters of the North Pacific Ocean. Sea otters play a crucial role in maintaining the health of kelp forest ecosystems by preying on sea urchins. Without sea otters, sea urchin populations can explode, leading to the overgrazing of kelp forests. This not only reduces habitat complexity but also affects the numerous species that rely on kelp forests for food and shelter. The presence of sea otters helps regulate sea urchin populations, allowing kelp forests to thrive and support a diverse array of marine life.

In terrestrial ecosystems, the African elephant serves as a keystone species in savanna and forest environments. Elephants are known as "ecosystem engineers" due to their ability to modify their habitat. By uprooting trees and shrubs, elephants create open spaces that promote the growth of grasses and other vegetation, supporting herbivores such as zebras and antelopes. Their dung also acts as a fertilizer, enriching the soil and promoting plant growth. The loss of elephants can lead to changes in vegetation structure, affecting the entire ecosystem and the species that depend on it.

The concept of keystone species extends to the plant kingdom as well. In the tropical rainforests of Central and South America, fig trees are considered keystone species due to their role as a critical food source for a wide range of animals. Fig trees produce fruit year-round, providing sustenance for birds, mammals, and insects during times when other food sources are scarce. The presence of fig trees helps maintain animal populations and supports the complex web of interactions within the rainforest ecosystem.

The importance of keystone species is further illustrated by the reintroduction of wolves to Yellowstone National Park in the United States. Wolves, as apex predators, help regulate the populations of herbivores such as elk. Before their reintroduction, elk populations had grown unchecked, leading to overgrazing and the degradation of vegetation along riverbanks. The return of wolves has helped restore balance to the ecosystem, allowing vegetation to recover and benefiting other species, such as beavers and songbirds, that rely on healthy riparian habitats.

The loss of keystone species can have profound and lasting effects on ecosystems. When a keystone species is removed, the balance of interactions within the ecosystem is disrupted, leading to changes in species composition and abundance. This can result in the loss of biodiversity, reduced ecosystem resilience, and diminished ecosystem services. The decline of keystone species is often driven by human activities, such as habitat destruction, pollution, and overexploitation, highlighting the need for conservation efforts to protect these vital components of ecosystems.

Conservation strategies that focus on keystone species can have far-reaching benefits for ecosystems and biodiversity. By protecting keystone species and their habitats, conservation efforts can help maintain the ecological processes and interactions that support a wide range of species. This approach can also enhance ecosystem resilience, making ecosystems more adaptable to environmental changes and disturbances.

The role of policy and governance in keystone species conservation is crucial. National and international policies that support the protection of keystone species and their habitats are essential for driving meaningful change. Initiatives such as the Endangered Species Act and the Convention on Biological Diversity aim to safeguard keystone species and promote sustainable development. However, the success of these initiatives depends on the commitment and cooperation of governments, businesses, and individuals.

Education and awareness are also vital components of efforts to conserve keystone species. By fostering a deeper understanding of the importance of keystone species and the consequences of their loss, individuals and communities can make informed choices that support sustainability. Environmental education programs, community-based conservation initiatives, and public awareness campaigns can empower people to take action and advocate for change.

Food Chains and Food Webs

In the vast and intricate tapestry of life, food chains and food webs serve as the fundamental frameworks that illustrate the flow of energy and nutrients through ecosystems. These interconnected systems reveal the complex relationships between organisms, highlighting the delicate balance that sustains life on Earth. Understanding food chains and food webs is essential for grasping the dynamics of ecosystems and the roles that different species play within them.

At the most basic level, a food chain is a linear sequence that depicts the transfer of energy from one organism to another. It begins with primary producers, typically plants or algae, which harness energy from the sun through photosynthesis. These producers form the foundation of the food chain, providing energy and nutrients to primary consumers, or herbivores, that feed on them. Secondary consumers, or carnivores, prey on herbivores, while tertiary consumers occupy the top of the food chain, feeding on other carnivores. Decomposers, such as fungi and bacteria, play a crucial role in breaking down dead organic matter, recycling nutrients back into the ecosystem and completing the cycle.

While food chains provide a simplified view of energy flow, they rarely exist in isolation. In reality, ecosystems are characterized by complex networks of interconnected food chains, known as food webs. These webs illustrate the myriad feeding relationships that occur within an ecosystem, capturing the diversity and complexity of interactions among species. Food webs demonstrate that most organisms have multiple food sources and predators, highlighting the interconnectedness and interdependence of species within an ecosystem.

The structure of food webs can vary significantly between ecosystems, influenced by factors such as habitat type, climate, and species diversity. In a forest ecosystem, for example, a food web might include trees as primary producers, supporting a variety of herbivores such as deer, insects, and birds. These herbivores, in turn, provide sustenance for predators like wolves, foxes, and raptors. Decomposers, including fungi and detritivores, break down leaf litter and fallen trees, returning nutrients to the soil and supporting the growth of new vegetation.

In aquatic ecosystems, food webs often begin with phytoplankton, microscopic algae that serve as primary producers. Zooplankton, small aquatic animals, feed on phytoplankton and are consumed by larger organisms such as fish and marine mammals. Apex predators, such as sharks and orcas, occupy the top of the food web, preying on a variety of species. The complexity of aquatic food webs is further enhanced by the presence of detrital food chains, where organic matter from dead plants and animals is consumed by detritivores and decomposers.

The stability and resilience of ecosystems are closely linked to the complexity of their food webs. Diverse food webs with multiple pathways for energy flow tend to be more resilient to disturbances, as the loss of one species can be compensated by others that fulfill similar ecological roles. This redundancy provides a buffer against environmental changes, helping ecosystems maintain their functions and services. Conversely, simplified food webs with fewer species and connections are more vulnerable to disruptions, as the loss of a single species can have cascading effects throughout the ecosystem. activities can have profound impacts on food chains and food webs, often leading to imbalances and disruptions. Overfishing, for example, can deplete populations of key species, altering the structure of marine food webs and affecting the entire ecosystem. Habitat destruction and pollution can reduce biodiversity, simplifying food webs and making ecosystems more susceptible to disturbances. The introduction of invasive species can also disrupt food webs by outcompeting native species and altering feeding relationships.

Conservation efforts aimed at preserving biodiversity and ecosystem health are essential for maintaining the integrity of food webs. Protecting habitats, regulating resource use, and restoring degraded ecosystems can help support diverse and resilient food webs. Conservation strategies that focus on keystone species, which play critical roles in maintaining the structure of food webs, can have far-reaching benefits for ecosystem stability and biodiversity.

Education and awareness are vital components of efforts to protect food webs and the ecosystems they support. By fostering a deeper understanding of the importance of food chains and food webs, individuals and communities can make informed choices that support sustainability. Environmental education programs, community-based conservation initiatives, and public awareness campaigns can empower people to take action and advocate for change.

Human Dependency on Ecosystem Services

Human existence is intricately intertwined with the natural world, relying on a vast array of ecosystem services that sustain life and enhance well-being. These services, provided by healthy ecosystems, are the foundation upon which societies are built, offering everything from the air we breathe to the food we consume. Understanding the depth of human dependency on these services is crucial for recognizing the importance of preserving and restoring ecosystems in the face of growing environmental challenges.

Ecosystem services are typically categorized into four main types: provisioning, regulating, cultural, and supporting services. Each category encompasses a range of benefits that ecosystems provide, directly or indirectly, to human societies. Provisioning services are perhaps the most tangible, as they include the resources that humans extract from nature for survival and economic activities. These resources encompass food, water, timber, fiber, and medicinal plants. The agricultural systems that feed the global population are deeply rooted in the natural processes of pollination, nutrient cycling, and soil formation, all of which are vital ecosystem services.

Regulating services are the natural processes that help maintain environmental stability and resilience. These services include climate regulation, water purification, disease control, and pollination. Forests, for example, play a critical role in sequestering carbon dioxide, mitigating climate change, and regulating local climates. Wetlands act as natural water filters, removing pollutants and sediments from water bodies, while also providing flood control by absorbing excess rainfall. The presence of diverse species in ecosystems contributes to pest and disease regulation, reducing the need for chemical interventions in agriculture.

Cultural services encompass the non-material benefits that ecosystems provide, enriching human lives through recreation, spiritual fulfillment, and aesthetic appreciation. Natural landscapes, such as mountains, forests, and coastlines, offer opportunities for outdoor activities, tourism, and relaxation, contributing to physical and mental well-being. Many cultures have deep spiritual and historical connections to specific ecosystems, which shape their identities and traditions. The beauty and diversity of nature inspire art, literature, and scientific inquiry, fostering a sense of wonder and curiosity about the world.

Supporting services are the underlying processes that enable ecosystems to function and provide the other three types of services. These include nutrient cycling, soil formation, primary production, and habitat provision. While supporting services may not have direct economic value, they are essential for the sustainability of ecosystems and the services they provide. For instance, the decomposition of organic matter by microorganisms recycles nutrients, maintaining soil fertility and supporting plant growth. The complex interactions between species within ecosystems create habitats that support biodiversity, which in turn enhances ecosystem resilience and productivity.

The dependency of human societies on ecosystem services is profound, yet often overlooked. As populations grow and economies expand, the demand for these services increases, placing immense pressure on ecosystems. Unsustainable practices, such as deforestation, overfishing, and pollution, degrade ecosystems and diminish their capacity to provide services. The loss of biodiversity further exacerbates this issue, as it reduces the resilience of ecosystems to adapt to environmental changes and disturbances.

The consequences of ecosystem degradation are far-reaching, affecting human health, livelihoods, and economies. The decline in pollinator populations, for example, poses a significant threat to global food security, as many crops rely on pollination for fruit and seed production. The loss of wetlands and forests reduces the natural capacity to regulate water cycles and mitigate climate change, leading to increased vulnerability to floods, droughts, and extreme weather events. The degradation of natural landscapes diminishes cultural and recreational opportunities, impacting quality of life and mental well-being.

Addressing the challenges of ecosystem degradation requires a multifaceted approach that integrates conservation, sustainable resource management, and policy interventions. Conservation efforts aim to protect and restore ecosystems, preserving their capacity to provide services. This can involve establishing protected areas, restoring degraded habitats, and promoting biodiversity-friendly practices in agriculture and forestry. Sustainable resource management seeks to balance human needs with the health of ecosystems, ensuring that resources are used efficiently and responsibly.

Policy interventions play a crucial role in supporting conservation and sustainable management efforts. National and international policies that promote ecosystem protection, climate change mitigation, and sustainable development are essential for driving meaningful change. Economic incentives, such as payments for ecosystem services and sustainable certification schemes, can encourage businesses and individuals to adopt practices that support ecosystem health. Collaborative governance, involving governments, communities, and stakeholders, is vital for ensuring that policies are effectively implemented and adapted to local contexts.

Education and awareness are also key components of efforts to address ecosystem degradation and promote sustainable practices. By fostering a deeper understanding of the importance of ecosystem services and the consequences of their loss, individuals and communities can make informed choices that support sustainability. Environmental education programs, community-based conservation initiatives, and public awareness campaigns can empower people to take action and advocate for change.

Case Studies Successful Ecosystem Management

In the realm of environmental conservation, successful ecosystem management stands as a beacon of hope, demonstrating that with the right strategies and commitment, the balance between human needs and ecological health can be achieved. Examining case studies of successful ecosystem management provides valuable insights into the practices and principles that contribute to sustainable outcomes. These stories of triumph highlight the importance of collaboration, innovation, and adaptability in addressing the complex challenges facing ecosystems worldwide.

One notable example of successful ecosystem management is the restoration of the Chesapeake Bay in the United States. Once a thriving estuary, the Chesapeake Bay faced severe degradation due to pollution, overfishing, and habitat loss. By the late 20th century, the bay's health had declined significantly, prompting a concerted effort to restore its ecosystems. The Chesapeake Bay Program, a regional partnership involving states, federal agencies, and local communities, was established to coordinate restoration efforts. Through a combination of pollution reduction measures, habitat restoration, and sustainable fisheries management, the program has made significant progress in improving water quality and restoring vital habitats such as wetlands and oyster reefs. The success of the Chesapeake Bay restoration underscores the importance of collaborative governance and the integration of science-based strategies in ecosystem management.

Another inspiring case study is the rewilding of the Scottish Highlands, a project aimed at restoring the region's natural ecosystems and biodiversity. The Highlands, once home to diverse wildlife and rich habitats, had suffered from centuries of deforestation, overgrazing, and human intervention. Rewilding efforts, led by organizations such as Trees for Life and the Scottish Rewilding Alliance, focus on reforesting the landscape, reintroducing native species, and promoting sustainable land use practices. The reintroduction of species like the Eurasian beaver has played a crucial role in restoring natural hydrological processes and enhancing habitat diversity. The project has not only revitalized the Highlands' ecosystems but also provided economic opportunities through ecotourism and sustainable agriculture, demonstrating the potential for rewilding to benefit both nature and local communities.

In the marine realm, the Great Barrier Reef Marine Park in Australia serves as a model of successful ecosystem management. The Great Barrier Reef, the world's largest coral reef system, faces numerous threats, including climate change, pollution, and overfishing. To protect this iconic ecosystem, the Australian government established the Great Barrier Reef Marine Park Authority, which implements a comprehensive management plan to safeguard the reef's biodiversity and ecological integrity. Key strategies include zoning regulations to control human activities, monitoring programs to assess reef health, and initiatives to reduce land-based pollution. The involvement of Indigenous communities in management decisions has also been instrumental in incorporating traditional knowledge and practices into conservation efforts. While challenges remain, the Great Barrier Reef Marine Park exemplifies the effectiveness of adaptive management and stakeholder engagement in preserving marine ecosystems.

The restoration of the Loess Plateau in China is another remarkable example of successful ecosystem management. The Loess Plateau, once a fertile region, had become severely degraded due to unsustainable agricultural practices and deforestation. In the 1990s, the Chinese government launched a large-scale restoration project to combat soil erosion and restore the plateau's ecosystems. The project involved reforestation, terracing, and the implementation of sustainable land management practices. As a result, vegetation cover increased, soil erosion was significantly reduced, and agricultural productivity improved. The Loess Plateau restoration has transformed the landscape and improved the livelihoods of local communities, highlighting the potential for ecosystem restoration to address both environmental and socio-economic challenges.

In Africa, the management of the Maasai Mara National Reserve in Kenya offers valuable lessons in balancing conservation and community needs. The Maasai Mara, renowned for its rich biodiversity and annual wildebeest migration, faces pressures from tourism, poaching, and land-use changes. The Maasai Mara Wildlife Conservancies Association, a partnership between local landowners and conservation organizations, has developed a model that integrates wildlife conservation with community development. By establishing conservancies on private lands, the initiative provides financial incentives to landowners for conservation efforts while supporting sustainable tourism and community projects. This approach has led to increased wildlife populations, improved habitat protection, and enhanced community benefits, demonstrating the importance of community-based conservation in achieving sustainable outcomes.

These case studies illustrate that successful ecosystem management requires a holistic approach that considers ecological, social, and economic factors. Key principles that emerge from these examples include the importance of collaboration among stakeholders, the integration of scientific knowledge and traditional practices, and the need for adaptive management to respond to changing conditions. By fostering partnerships and engaging local communities, ecosystem management efforts can build resilience and ensure the long-term sustainability of natural resources.

Chapter 3

Human Needs and Environmental Resources

The Essentials Water, Air, and Soil

Water, air, and soil are the fundamental elements that sustain life on Earth, forming the bedrock of ecosystems and supporting the intricate web of interactions among living organisms. These essentials are interconnected, each playing a vital role in maintaining ecological balance and providing the resources necessary for survival. Understanding the significance of water, air, and soil is crucial for appreciating their contributions to ecosystems and the importance of preserving their quality and availability.

Water is the lifeblood of ecosystems, a critical component that supports all forms of life. It serves as a habitat for countless aquatic species, from the smallest microorganisms to the largest marine mammals. In terrestrial ecosystems, water is essential for plant growth, providing the medium through which nutrients are absorbed and transported. The availability and quality of water influence the distribution and abundance of species, shaping the structure and function of ecosystems.

The hydrological cycle, or water cycle, is the continuous movement of water through the Earth's atmosphere, surface, and subsurface. This cycle is driven by solar energy, which causes water to evaporate from oceans, lakes, and rivers, forming clouds that eventually release precipitation. Precipitation replenishes freshwater sources, such as rivers, lakes, and aquifers, which are vital for human consumption, agriculture, and industry. The water cycle also plays a crucial role in regulating climate, as it influences temperature and weather patterns. activities, however, have significantly impacted the availability and quality of water resources. Pollution from industrial, agricultural, and domestic sources contaminates water bodies, affecting the health of aquatic ecosystems and the species that depend on them. Over-extraction of water for irrigation, industry, and urban use depletes freshwater sources, leading to water scarcity and conflicts over access. Climate change exacerbates these challenges by altering precipitation patterns and increasing the frequency of extreme weather events, such as droughts and floods.

Air, the invisible yet indispensable element, is the medium through which life-sustaining gases are exchanged. The Earth's atmosphere is composed primarily of nitrogen and oxygen, with trace amounts of other gases, such as carbon dioxide and methane. These gases are essential for processes like photosynthesis and respiration, which underpin the energy flow in ecosystems. The atmosphere also acts as a protective shield, filtering harmful solar radiation and regulating the planet's temperature through the greenhouse effect.

Air quality is a critical factor in ecosystem health, as pollutants can have detrimental effects on both terrestrial and aquatic environments. Emissions from vehicles, industries, and agriculture release pollutants such as sulfur dioxide, nitrogen oxides, and particulate matter into the atmosphere. These pollutants can lead to acid rain, which damages vegetation, soils, and aquatic habitats. Airborne pollutants also contribute to the formation of ground-level ozone, a harmful gas that affects plant growth and reduces agricultural productivity.

Efforts to improve air quality focus on reducing emissions through cleaner technologies, regulatory measures, and sustainable practices. Transitioning to renewable energy sources, such as solar and wind power, can significantly reduce air pollution and mitigate climate change. Implementing stricter emissions standards for vehicles and industries, along with promoting public transportation and energy efficiency, can further enhance air quality and protect ecosystems.

Soil, often overlooked, is the foundation of terrestrial ecosystems, providing the medium for plant growth and supporting a diverse array of organisms. It is a complex mixture of minerals, organic matter, water, and air, formed over millennia through the weathering of rocks and the decomposition of organic material. Soil fertility is a key determinant of ecosystem productivity, as it influences the availability of nutrients for plants and the organisms that depend on them.

Healthy soils perform a range of essential functions, including nutrient cycling, water filtration, and carbon storage. They support biodiversity by providing habitat for countless microorganisms, insects, and other organisms that contribute to ecosystem processes. Soils also play a crucial role in regulating the Earth's climate, as they store significant amounts of carbon and influence the exchange of greenhouse gases with the atmosphere.

Human activities, however, pose significant threats to soil health. Unsustainable agricultural practices, such as monoculture, overgrazing, and excessive use of chemical fertilizers and pesticides, degrade soil structure and reduce fertility. Deforestation and land conversion for agriculture and urban development lead to soil erosion, loss of organic matter, and desertification. These processes not only diminish the productivity of ecosystems but also contribute to climate change by releasing stored carbon into the atmosphere.

Efforts to protect and restore soil health focus on sustainable land management practices that enhance soil fertility and prevent degradation. Techniques such as crop rotation, agroforestry, and conservation tillage can improve soil structure, increase organic matter, and reduce erosion. Restoring degraded lands through reforestation and revegetation can enhance soil health and contribute to carbon sequestration, mitigating climate change.

The interconnectedness of water, air, and soil underscores the need for integrated approaches to ecosystem management and conservation. Protecting these essentials requires a holistic understanding of their interactions and the impacts of human activities. Collaborative efforts involving governments, communities, and stakeholders are crucial for developing and implementing effective strategies to preserve and restore these vital resources.

Education and awareness are also key components of efforts to protect water, air, and soil. By fostering a deeper understanding of the importance of these essentials and the consequences of their degradation, individuals and communities can make informed choices that support sustainability. Environmental education programs, community-based conservation initiatives, and public awareness campaigns can empower people to take action and advocate for change.

Agriculture and Food Security

Agriculture has been the cornerstone of human civilization, providing the sustenance necessary for societies to flourish and evolve. As the global population continues to rise, the challenge of ensuring food security becomes increasingly pressing. Food security, defined as the availability of food and individuals' access to it, is a complex issue influenced by a myriad of factors, including agricultural practices, climate change, economic policies, and social dynamics. Understanding the interplay between agriculture and food security is essential for developing strategies that can sustainably meet the nutritional needs of a growing world.

The evolution of agriculture has been marked by significant advancements, from the domestication of plants and animals to the development of modern farming techniques. These innovations have dramatically increased food production, enabling societies to support larger populations. However, the intensification of agriculture has also led to environmental challenges, such as soil degradation, water scarcity, and loss of biodiversity. Balancing the need for increased food production with the preservation of natural resources is a critical aspect of achieving food security.

Sustainable agriculture practices offer a pathway to enhancing food security while minimizing environmental impacts. These practices focus on maintaining soil health, conserving water, and promoting biodiversity. Crop rotation, for example, involves alternating the types of crops grown on a piece of land to improve soil fertility and reduce pest and disease pressures. Agroforestry, which integrates trees and shrubs into agricultural landscapes, can enhance biodiversity, improve soil structure, and provide additional sources of income for farmers.

Water management is another crucial component of sustainable agriculture. Efficient irrigation systems, such as drip irrigation, can significantly reduce water use while maintaining crop yields. Rainwater harvesting and the use of drought-resistant crop varieties can also help farmers adapt to changing climate conditions and reduce their reliance on external water sources. By implementing these practices, farmers can enhance their resilience to climate variability and ensure a stable food supply.

The role of technology in agriculture cannot be overstated. Advances in biotechnology, precision agriculture, and digital tools have the potential to revolutionize food production. Genetically modified crops, for instance, can be engineered to resist pests, tolerate harsh environmental conditions, and improve nutritional content. Precision agriculture uses data and technology to optimize field-level management, allowing farmers to apply inputs such as water, fertilizers, and pesticides more efficiently. These innovations can increase productivity, reduce waste, and contribute to food security.

However, the adoption of new technologies must be approached with caution, considering potential risks and ethical concerns. The use of genetically modified organisms (GMOs) has sparked debates over food safety, environmental impacts, and the rights of farmers. Ensuring that technological advancements are accessible to smallholder farmers, who produce a significant portion of the world's food, is also crucial for equitable food security. Policies that support research, education, and infrastructure development can help bridge the gap between technological potential and practical application.

Economic and social factors play a significant role in shaping food security. Access to markets, credit, and education can empower farmers to improve their livelihoods and contribute to a stable food supply. Strengthening rural infrastructure, such as roads, storage facilities, and communication networks, can enhance market access and reduce post-harvest losses. Social safety nets and nutrition programs can provide vulnerable populations with the resources they need to achieve food security.

Climate change poses a formidable challenge to agriculture and food security, as it affects weather patterns, water availability, and the prevalence of pests and diseases. Adapting to these changes requires a multifaceted approach that includes developing climate-resilient crops, improving water management, and diversifying agricultural systems. Building the capacity of farmers to adapt to climate change through training, extension services, and access to climate information is essential for ensuring food security in a changing world.

International cooperation and policy frameworks are vital for addressing the global nature of food security challenges. Initiatives such as the United Nations' Sustainable Development Goals (SDGs) and the Paris Agreement on climate change provide a platform for countries to collaborate on sustainable agriculture and food security. Trade policies that promote fair and equitable access to food markets can also contribute to global food security by ensuring that food surpluses reach regions in need.

Community-based approaches to agriculture and food security can empower local populations to take charge of their food systems. By involving communities in decision-making processes, these approaches can ensure that agricultural practices are tailored to local needs and conditions. Community-supported agriculture (CSA) programs, for example, connect consumers directly with local farmers, fostering a sense of shared responsibility for food production and consumption.

Education and awareness are key components of efforts to enhance food security. By fostering a deeper understanding of the importance of sustainable agriculture and the challenges of food security, individuals and communities can make informed choices that support sustainability. Educational programs, public awareness campaigns, and community initiatives can empower people to take action and advocate for change.

Energy Consumption and Its Ecological Impact

Energy consumption is a defining feature of modern society, powering everything from the lights in our homes to the industries that drive economic growth. However, the ecological impact of energy consumption is profound, influencing climate patterns, biodiversity, and the health of ecosystems worldwide. Understanding the relationship between energy use and ecological consequences is crucial for developing strategies that balance human needs with environmental sustainability.

The industrial revolution marked a turning point in human history, ushering in an era of unprecedented energy consumption. Fossil fuels—coal, oil, and natural gas—became the primary sources of energy, fueling industrial processes, transportation, and electricity generation. While these energy sources have driven economic development and improved living standards, they have also contributed to significant environmental challenges.

One of the most pressing ecological impacts of energy consumption is climate change. The burning of fossil fuels releases greenhouse gases, such as carbon dioxide and methane, into the atmosphere. These gases trap heat, leading to global warming and altering climate patterns. The consequences of climate change are far-reaching, affecting weather systems, sea levels, and the distribution of species. Ecosystems struggle to adapt to these rapid changes, resulting in shifts in biodiversity and the loss of habitats.

Air pollution is another significant ecological impact of energy consumption. The combustion of fossil fuels releases pollutants, including sulfur dioxide, nitrogen oxides, and particulate matter, into the atmosphere. These pollutants can lead to the formation of smog and acid rain, which harm vegetation, soil, and water bodies. Air pollution also poses health risks to humans and wildlife, contributing to respiratory diseases and reducing life expectancy.

The extraction and transportation of fossil fuels have direct ecological consequences as well. Oil spills, coal mining, and natural gas extraction can lead to habitat destruction, soil and water contamination, and the disruption of ecosystems. The construction of infrastructure, such as pipelines and roads, fragments habitats and alters landscapes, affecting the movement and survival of species.

Transitioning to renewable energy sources offers a pathway to reducing the ecological impact of energy consumption. Renewable energy, derived from natural processes that are replenished constantly, includes solar, wind, hydroelectric, and geothermal power. These sources produce little to no greenhouse gas emissions and have a lower environmental footprint compared to fossil fuels.

Solar energy harnesses the power of the sun through photovoltaic cells or solar thermal systems. It is a clean and abundant energy source that can be deployed at various scales, from residential rooftops to large solar farms. Wind energy, generated by wind turbines, is another renewable option that has gained traction in recent years. Wind farms can be located onshore or offshore, providing a flexible and scalable energy solution.

Hydroelectric power, generated by the flow of water through turbines, is one of the oldest and most widely used forms of renewable energy. While it is a reliable and efficient energy source, the construction of dams can have ecological impacts, such as altering river ecosystems and affecting fish migration. Geothermal energy, derived from the Earth's internal heat, offers a stable and sustainable energy source with minimal environmental impact.

The transition to renewable energy requires investment in infrastructure, technology, and policy frameworks. Governments, businesses, and communities play a crucial role in supporting this transition through incentives, research and development, and public awareness campaigns. Policies that promote energy efficiency, carbon pricing, and renewable energy targets can drive the adoption of clean energy technologies and reduce reliance on fossil fuels.

Energy efficiency is a key component of reducing the ecological impact of energy consumption. By using energy more efficiently, we can reduce demand and minimize environmental impacts. Energy-efficient technologies, such as LED lighting, high-efficiency appliances, and advanced building materials, can significantly reduce energy use in homes and businesses. Implementing energy management systems and practices in industries can also enhance efficiency and reduce emissions.

Behavioral changes and lifestyle choices can contribute to energy conservation and sustainability. Simple actions, such as turning off lights when not in use, using public transportation, and reducing waste, can collectively make a significant difference. Education and awareness are essential for empowering individuals and communities to make informed choices that support energy sustainability.

The ecological impact of energy consumption is a global challenge that requires collective action and collaboration. International agreements, such as the Paris Agreement, provide a framework for countries to work together to reduce greenhouse gas emissions and promote sustainable energy practices. By sharing knowledge, technology, and resources, countries can accelerate the transition to a low-carbon future and mitigate the ecological impacts of energy consumption.

Urbanization and Land Use

Urbanization is a defining characteristic of the modern era, reshaping landscapes and transforming the way people live, work, and interact. As cities expand and populations grow, the demand for land intensifies, leading to significant changes in land use patterns. Understanding the dynamics of urbanization and its impact on land use is crucial for developing sustainable strategies that balance development with environmental preservation.

The process of urbanization involves the migration of people from rural to urban areas, driven by factors such as economic opportunities, access to services, and improved living standards. This migration fuels the growth of cities, resulting in the expansion of urban areas and the conversion of natural and agricultural lands into residential, commercial, and industrial zones. While urbanization can drive economic growth and innovation, it also poses challenges related to land use, infrastructure, and environmental sustainability.

One of the most visible impacts of urbanization is the loss of natural habitats and agricultural lands. As cities expand, forests, wetlands, and farmlands are often cleared to make way for new developments. This land conversion can lead to habitat fragmentation, loss of biodiversity, and disruption of ecosystem services, such as water filtration and carbon sequestration. The loss of agricultural land also raises concerns about food security, as it reduces the capacity for local food production and increases reliance on imported goods.

Urban sprawl, characterized by low-density development and the spread of urban areas into surrounding regions, exacerbates the challenges of land use. Sprawl often leads to inefficient land use patterns, increased reliance on automobiles, and higher infrastructure costs. It can also contribute to social and economic disparities, as access to services and amenities may be unevenly distributed across sprawling urban landscapes.

To address the challenges of urbanization and land use, planners and policymakers are increasingly turning to the concept of smart growth. Smart growth emphasizes sustainable development practices that promote compact, mixed-use, and transit-oriented communities. By focusing on efficient land use, smart growth aims to reduce the environmental footprint of urban areas while enhancing quality of life for residents.

One key principle of smart growth is the promotion of higher-density development, which can help preserve open spaces and reduce the need for new infrastructure. By encouraging the development of multi-story buildings and mixed-use neighborhoods, cities can accommodate growing populations without expanding their physical footprint. This approach also supports the creation of vibrant, walkable communities where residents have easy access to jobs, services, and recreational opportunities.

Public transportation plays a crucial role in supporting sustainable urbanization and land use. By investing in efficient and accessible transit systems, cities can reduce reliance on private vehicles, decrease traffic congestion, and lower greenhouse gas emissions. Transit-oriented development, which focuses on creating compact, walkable communities around transit hubs, can further enhance the benefits of public transportation and promote sustainable land use patterns.

Green infrastructure is another important component of sustainable urbanization. By integrating natural elements, such as parks, green roofs, and urban forests, into the urban fabric, cities can enhance ecosystem services, improve air and water quality, and provide recreational opportunities for residents.

Green infrastructure can also help mitigate the impacts of climate change by reducing urban heat island effects and managing stormwater runoff.

Community engagement and participatory planning are essential for successful urbanization and land use management. By involving residents in decision-making processes, planners can ensure that development reflects the needs and priorities of local communities. Participatory approaches can also foster a sense of ownership and stewardship, encouraging residents to take an active role in shaping the future of their neighborhoods.

Technological innovations offer new opportunities for managing urbanization and land use. Geographic information systems (GIS), remote sensing, and data analytics can provide valuable insights into land use patterns, infrastructure needs, and environmental impacts. By leveraging these tools, planners can make informed decisions and develop strategies that promote sustainable urban growth.

The integration of sustainable practices into urbanization and land use planning requires supportive policies and regulatory frameworks. Zoning regulations, building codes, and development incentives can encourage sustainable development and discourage sprawl. Policies that promote affordable housing, mixed-use development, and public transportation can also contribute to more equitable and sustainable urban environments.

Education and awareness are critical for fostering a culture of sustainability in urban areas. By raising awareness of the impacts of urbanization and the benefits of sustainable land use practices, individuals and communities can make informed choices that support environmental preservation and social well-being. Educational programs, public awareness campaigns, and community initiatives can empower people to take action and advocate for sustainable urban development.

Balancing Resource Extraction with Conservation

Resource extraction has been a driving force behind human progress, providing the raw materials necessary for infrastructure, technology, and economic development. From minerals and fossil fuels to timber and water, these resources are integral to modern life. However, the extraction process often comes at a significant environmental cost, threatening ecosystems and biodiversity. Balancing resource extraction with conservation is a complex challenge that requires innovative strategies and a commitment to sustainable practices.

The history of resource extraction is intertwined with the rise of industrialization and urbanization. As societies expanded, the demand for resources grew, leading to the development of mining, logging, and drilling industries. These activities have contributed to economic growth and improved living standards, but they have also resulted in habitat destruction, pollution, and the depletion of natural resources. The challenge lies in finding ways to meet human needs while preserving the ecological integrity of the planet.

Sustainable resource management is a key approach to balancing extraction with conservation. This involves using resources in a way that meets current needs without compromising the ability of future generations to meet their own. It requires a comprehensive understanding of the ecological, social, and economic impacts of resource extraction and the implementation of practices that minimize negative effects.

One of the fundamental principles of sustainable resource management is the conservation of biodiversity. Biodiversity, the variety of life on Earth, is essential for ecosystem resilience and the provision of ecosystem services, such as clean air and water, pollination, and climate regulation. Protecting biodiversity involves preserving habitats, maintaining genetic diversity, and preventing the overexploitation of species.

In the context of resource extraction, conservation efforts can take many forms. Protected areas, such as national parks and wildlife reserves, play a crucial role in safeguarding habitats and species from the impacts of extraction activities. These areas provide a refuge for wildlife and serve as important sites for scientific research and environmental education. However, the establishment of protected areas must be carefully planned to ensure that they are effectively managed and that local communities are involved in conservation efforts.

Another important aspect of balancing extraction with conservation is the adoption of sustainable extraction practices. In the mining industry, for example, techniques such as precision mining and the use of environmentally friendly technologies can reduce the environmental footprint of extraction activities. Reclamation and rehabilitation of mined lands can restore ecosystems and provide opportunities for new land uses, such as agriculture or recreation.

In the forestry sector, sustainable logging practices, such as selective logging and reduced-impact logging, can help maintain forest health and biodiversity. These practices involve carefully planning and executing logging operations to minimize damage to the surrounding environment. Reforestation and afforestation efforts can also contribute to conservation by restoring degraded lands and increasing carbon sequestration.

Water resource management is another critical component of sustainable extraction. The extraction of water for agriculture, industry, and domestic use can lead to the depletion of freshwater sources and the degradation of aquatic ecosystems. Sustainable water management involves optimizing water use efficiency, protecting water quality, and maintaining the ecological health of water bodies. Techniques such as rainwater harvesting, drip irrigation, and wastewater recycling can help reduce water consumption and preserve aquatic habitats.

Community involvement and stakeholder engagement are essential for successful resource management and conservation efforts. Local communities often have valuable knowledge and a vested interest in the sustainable use of natural resources. By involving communities in decision-making processes and providing them with the tools and resources needed to participate in conservation efforts, resource managers can build trust and foster a sense of ownership and responsibility.

Economic incentives and market-based approaches can also play a role in promoting sustainable resource extraction. Certification schemes, such as the Forest Stewardship Council (FSC) for timber and the Marine Stewardship Council (MSC) for seafood, provide consumers with information about the sustainability of products and encourage companies to adopt environmentally friendly practices. Payment for ecosystem services (PES) programs offer financial incentives to landowners and communities for conserving natural resources and maintaining ecosystem services.

Policy frameworks and regulatory measures are crucial for ensuring that resource extraction is conducted in a sustainable manner. Governments can implement policies that promote sustainable practices, such as setting limits on resource extraction, enforcing environmental standards, and supporting research and innovation. International agreements and collaborations can also facilitate the sharing of knowledge and resources and promote global efforts to balance extraction with conservation.

Education and awareness are key components of efforts to balance resource extraction with conservation. By raising awareness of the impacts of extraction activities and the importance of conservation, individuals and communities can make informed choices that support sustainability. Educational programs, public awareness campaigns, and community initiatives can empower people to take action and advocate for change.

Chapter 4

Climate Change and Its Ecological Implications

The Science of Climate Change

Climate change is one of the most pressing challenges of our time, with profound implications for the planet's ecosystems, weather patterns, and human societies. At its core, climate change refers to long-term alterations in temperature, precipitation, and other atmospheric conditions on Earth. These changes are driven by a complex interplay of natural processes and human activities, with the latter playing an increasingly dominant role in recent decades. Understanding the science behind climate change is essential for developing effective strategies to mitigate its impacts and adapt to its consequences.

The Earth's climate system is a dynamic and interconnected web of components, including the atmosphere, oceans, land surfaces, and ice masses. Solar radiation is the primary driver of the climate system, providing the energy that powers weather patterns and influences temperature. The balance between incoming solar radiation and outgoing infrared radiation determines the Earth's energy budget and, consequently, its climate.

Greenhouse gases (GHGs) play a crucial role in regulating the Earth's temperature by trapping heat in the atmosphere. This natural greenhouse effect is essential for maintaining a habitable climate, as it prevents the planet from losing too much heat to space. However, human activities, such as the burning of fossil fuels, deforestation, and industrial processes, have significantly increased the concentration of GHGs in the atmosphere. Carbon dioxide (CO_2), methane (CH_4), and nitrous oxide (N_2O) are among the most significant anthropogenic GHGs, contributing to the enhanced greenhouse effect and global warming.

The evidence for climate change is overwhelming and comes from a variety of sources. Instrumental records, such as temperature measurements and satellite data, provide direct evidence of rising global temperatures, shrinking ice sheets, and changing precipitation patterns. Paleoclimate data, derived from ice cores, tree rings, and sediment layers, offer insights into past climate conditions and help scientists understand the natural variability of the climate system.

Climate models are essential tools for understanding and predicting climate change. These complex computer simulations use mathematical equations to represent the interactions between different components of the climate system. By inputting data on GHG concentrations, solar radiation, and other factors, scientists can simulate past, present, and future climate conditions. Climate models have consistently shown that the observed warming trend over the past century is largely attributable to human activities, particularly the emission of GHGs.

The impacts of climate change are already being felt around the world, with significant consequences for ecosystems, weather patterns, and human societies.

Rising global temperatures are causing polar ice to melt and sea levels to rise, threatening coastal communities and ecosystems. Changes in precipitation patterns are leading to more frequent and intense droughts, floods, and storms, affecting agriculture, water resources, and infrastructure.

Ecosystems are particularly vulnerable to climate change, as they depend on specific climate conditions for their survival. Shifts in temperature and precipitation can alter the distribution of species, disrupt food webs, and lead to the loss of biodiversity. Coral reefs, for example, are highly sensitive to temperature changes and are experiencing widespread bleaching and mortality due to warming ocean waters. societies are also at risk from the impacts of climate change, with vulnerable populations facing the greatest challenges. Food security is threatened by changes in agricultural productivity, while water scarcity is exacerbated by altered precipitation patterns and increased evaporation. Health risks, such as heat-related illnesses and the spread of vector-borne diseases, are also on the rise. Additionally, climate change can exacerbate existing social and economic inequalities, leading to increased displacement and conflict.

Mitigating climate change requires a concerted effort to reduce GHG emissions and transition to a low-carbon economy. Renewable energy sources, such as solar, wind, and hydropower, offer a sustainable alternative to fossil fuels and can significantly reduce emissions. Energy efficiency measures, such as improving building insulation and adopting fuel-efficient technologies, can also contribute to emission reductions.

Carbon capture and storage (CCS) technologies hold promise for mitigating climate change by capturing CO_2 emissions from industrial processes and storing them underground. Reforestation and afforestation efforts can enhance carbon sequestration, as trees absorb CO_2 from the atmosphere and store it in their biomass. Protecting and restoring natural ecosystems, such as wetlands and mangroves, can also contribute to climate mitigation by enhancing carbon storage and providing additional ecosystem services.

Adaptation is another critical component of addressing climate change, as it involves adjusting to the impacts that are already occurring and preparing for future changes. Adaptation strategies can include building resilient infrastructure, implementing water management practices, and developing early warning systems for extreme weather events. Community-based adaptation approaches, which involve local populations in planning and decision-making, can enhance resilience and ensure that adaptation measures are culturally appropriate and effective.

International cooperation is essential for addressing the global nature of climate change. Agreements such as the Paris Agreement provide a framework for countries to work together to reduce emissions and promote sustainable development. By setting emission reduction targets and providing financial and technical support to developing countries, international agreements can facilitate global efforts to combat climate change.

Education and awareness are key components of efforts to address climate change. By raising awareness of the science and impacts of climate change, individuals and communities can make informed choices that support sustainability. Educational programs, public awareness campaigns, and community initiatives can empower people to take action and advocate for change.

Effects on Global Ecosystems

The intricate web of life that constitutes Earth's ecosystems is profoundly influenced by a myriad of factors, with climate change and human activities being among the most significant. These ecosystems, ranging from lush rainforests to arid deserts, are not only home to an incredible diversity of species but also provide essential services that sustain human life. Understanding the effects of environmental changes on global ecosystems is crucial for developing strategies to preserve biodiversity and maintain the health of our planet.

Ecosystems are dynamic entities, constantly adapting to changes in their environment. However, the rapid pace of human-induced changes poses unprecedented challenges. Climate change, driven by the accumulation of greenhouse gases in the atmosphere, is altering temperature and precipitation patterns worldwide. These changes have cascading effects on ecosystems, influencing species distribution, habitat availability, and the timing of biological events.

One of the most visible impacts of climate change on ecosystems is the shift in species ranges. As temperatures rise, many species are moving towards higher altitudes or latitudes in search of suitable habitats. This migration can lead to changes in community composition and interactions, as new species enter ecosystems and compete with established ones. For instance, in mountainous regions, species adapted to cooler climates may find themselves with nowhere to go as they reach the peaks, leading to potential extinctions.

Phenological changes, or shifts in the timing of biological events, are another consequence of climate change. Many species rely on specific environmental cues, such as temperature or daylight, to trigger activities like breeding, migration, or flowering. As these cues change, mismatches can occur between species and their environment. For example, if plants bloom earlier due to warmer temperatures, pollinators that rely on these plants may miss their food source, disrupting the entire food web.

Aquatic ecosystems are particularly vulnerable to the effects of climate change. Rising temperatures and altered precipitation patterns can lead to changes in water availability and quality, affecting freshwater and marine habitats. Coral reefs, often referred to as the "rainforests of the sea," are experiencing widespread bleaching due to increased sea temperatures. This bleaching weakens corals, making them more susceptible to disease and reducing their ability to support diverse marine life.

Ocean acidification, a result of increased carbon dioxide absorption by seawater, poses another threat to marine ecosystems. As the pH of ocean water decreases, it becomes more difficult for organisms like corals, mollusks, and some plankton species to build and maintain their calcium carbonate shells and skeletons. This can have far-reaching effects on marine food webs and the communities that depend on them.

Terrestrial ecosystems are not immune to the impacts of climate change. Forests, which play a crucial role in carbon sequestration and climate regulation, are facing increased risks from pests, diseases, and wildfires. Warmer temperatures and prolonged droughts can weaken trees, making them more susceptible to infestations and reducing their ability to recover from disturbances. The loss of forests not only affects biodiversity but also contributes to the release of stored carbon, exacerbating climate change. activities, such as deforestation, urbanization, and agriculture, further compound the challenges faced by ecosystems. Habitat destruction and fragmentation reduce the available space for species to thrive, leading to declines in biodiversity. Pollution, including plastic waste, pesticides, and industrial runoff, contaminates ecosystems and poses health risks to both wildlife and humans.

Conservation efforts are essential for mitigating the impacts of environmental changes on ecosystems. Protected areas, such as national parks and wildlife reserves, provide refuges for species and help maintain ecological processes. However, these areas must be effectively managed and connected through ecological corridors to allow species to move and adapt to changing conditions.

Restoration ecology offers another avenue for supporting ecosystems in the face of change. By restoring degraded habitats and reintroducing native species, we can enhance ecosystem resilience and function. Restoration projects can range from reforestation efforts to the rehabilitation of wetlands and grasslands, each tailored to the specific needs and conditions of the ecosystem.

Community involvement is crucial for the success of conservation and restoration initiatives. Local communities often have a deep understanding of their environment and can play a vital role in protecting and managing natural resources. By involving communities in decision-making processes and providing them with the tools and resources needed to participate in conservation efforts, we can build a sense of ownership and stewardship.

Education and awareness are key components of efforts to protect global ecosystems. By raising awareness of the impacts of environmental changes and the importance of biodiversity, individuals and communities can make informed choices that support sustainability. Educational programs, public awareness campaigns, and community initiatives can empower people to take action and advocate for change.

International cooperation is essential for addressing the global nature of ecosystem challenges. Agreements such as the Convention on Biological Diversity provide a framework for countries to work together to conserve biodiversity and promote sustainable development. By sharing knowledge, resources, and best practices, countries can enhance their capacity to protect ecosystems and address the drivers of environmental change.

Human Contributions to Climate Change

Human activities have significantly altered the Earth's climate system, contributing to the phenomenon known as climate change. This transformation is largely driven by the emission of greenhouse gases (GHGs) and other pollutants, which have increased dramatically since the onset of the industrial revolution. Understanding the human contributions to climate change is essential for developing effective strategies to mitigate its impacts and transition to a more sustainable future.

The industrial revolution marked a turning point in human history, as societies began to harness the power of fossil fuels—coal, oil, and natural gas—to drive economic growth and technological advancement. These energy sources, while abundant and efficient, release large quantities of carbon dioxide (CO_2) and other GHGs when burned. As a result, the concentration of CO_2 in the atmosphere has risen from approximately 280 parts per million (ppm) in pre-industrial times to over 400 ppm today, a level not seen in millions of years.

The burning of fossil fuels is the largest single source of human-induced GHG emissions, accounting for the majority of CO_2 released into the atmosphere. Power generation, transportation, and industrial processes are the primary contributors, as they rely heavily on fossil fuels for energy. The combustion of coal, in particular, is a major source of CO_2 emissions, as well as other pollutants such as sulfur dioxide (SO_2) and nitrogen oxides (NOx), which contribute to air pollution and acid rain.

Transportation is another significant contributor to GHG emissions, with cars, trucks, airplanes, and ships all relying on fossil fuels for propulsion. The rapid growth of global trade and travel has led to an increase in transportation-related emissions, further exacerbating climate change. Efforts to reduce these emissions include the development of fuel-efficient vehicles, the promotion of public transportation, and the adoption of alternative fuels such as electricity and hydrogen.

Industrial processes, such as cement production, steel manufacturing, and chemical synthesis, also contribute to GHG emissions. These processes often involve the release of CO_2 and other gases, such as methane (CH_4) and nitrous oxide (N_2O), as byproducts. Methane, in particular, is a potent greenhouse gas with a global warming potential many times greater than that of CO_2. It is released during the extraction and transportation of fossil fuels, as well as from agricultural activities and waste management.

Agriculture is a significant source of GHG emissions, contributing to climate change through the release of methane and nitrous oxide. Livestock production, particularly cattle, generates methane through enteric fermentation, a digestive process that occurs in the stomachs of ruminant animals. Rice paddies, which are flooded fields used for growing rice, also produce methane as organic matter decomposes in anaerobic conditions. Additionally, the use of synthetic fertilizers in agriculture leads to the release of nitrous oxide, a greenhouse gas with a warming potential even greater than methane.

Deforestation and land-use change are critical factors in human contributions to climate change. Forests act as carbon sinks, absorbing CO2 from the atmosphere and storing it in biomass. When forests are cleared for agriculture, urban development, or logging, this stored carbon is released back into the atmosphere, contributing to global warming. Deforestation also reduces the Earth's capacity to absorb CO2, further exacerbating the problem.

Urbanization and the expansion of cities contribute to climate change through increased energy consumption, transportation emissions, and changes in land use. The construction and operation of buildings account for a significant portion of global energy use and CO2 emissions. Urban areas also generate heat, known as the urban heat island effect, which can exacerbate local climate conditions and increase energy demand for cooling.

Waste management practices, such as landfilling and incineration, contribute to GHG emissions through the release of methane and CO2. Organic waste decomposing in landfills produces methane, while the burning of waste materials releases CO2 and other pollutants. Efforts to reduce waste-related emissions include recycling, composting, and the capture and utilization of landfill gas for energy.

Addressing human contributions to climate change requires a multifaceted approach that involves reducing GHG emissions, enhancing carbon sinks, and transitioning to sustainable practices. Renewable energy sources, such as solar, wind, and hydropower, offer a viable alternative to fossil fuels and can significantly reduce emissions. Energy efficiency measures, such as improving building insulation and adopting energy-efficient appliances, can also contribute to emission reductions.

Sustainable agriculture practices, such as precision farming, agroforestry, and organic farming, can help reduce emissions from the agricultural sector. These practices focus on optimizing resource use, enhancing soil health, and reducing the reliance on synthetic fertilizers and pesticides. Reforestation and afforestation efforts can enhance carbon sequestration and restore degraded lands, while protecting existing forests is crucial for maintaining the Earth's carbon balance.

Policy frameworks and regulatory measures play a critical role in addressing human contributions to climate change. Governments can implement policies that promote sustainable practices, such as setting emission reduction targets, enforcing environmental standards, and providing incentives for renewable energy and energy efficiency. International agreements, such as the Paris Agreement, provide a framework for countries to work together to reduce emissions and promote sustainable development.

Education and awareness are essential for fostering a culture of sustainability and encouraging individuals and communities to take action. By raising awareness of the human contributions to climate change and the importance of reducing emissions, people can make informed choices that support sustainability. Educational programs, public awareness campaigns, and community initiatives can empower individuals to advocate for change and adopt sustainable practices in their daily lives.

Mitigation and Adaptation Strategies

Addressing the challenges posed by climate change requires a dual approach: mitigation and adaptation. These strategies are essential for reducing greenhouse gas emissions and enhancing the resilience of communities and ecosystems to the impacts of climate change. While mitigation focuses on addressing the root causes of climate change, adaptation involves adjusting to its effects. Together, they form a comprehensive framework for tackling this global issue.

Mitigation strategies aim to reduce or prevent the emission of greenhouse gases, thereby limiting the extent of climate change. One of the most effective ways to achieve this is through the transition to renewable energy sources. Solar, wind, and hydropower offer sustainable alternatives to fossil fuels, which are the primary contributors to carbon dioxide emissions. By investing in renewable energy infrastructure and technology, countries can significantly reduce their carbon footprint and promote energy security.

Energy efficiency is another critical component of mitigation efforts. By optimizing energy use in buildings, transportation, and industry, we can reduce emissions and lower energy costs. Simple measures, such as improving insulation, using energy-efficient appliances, and adopting smart grid technologies, can have a substantial impact. Additionally, promoting public transportation, carpooling, and the use of electric vehicles can reduce emissions from the transportation sector.

Carbon capture and storage (CCS) technologies offer a promising solution for mitigating emissions from industrial processes and power generation. These technologies capture carbon dioxide emissions at their source and store them underground, preventing them from entering the atmosphere. While CCS is still in the early stages of development, it has the potential to play a significant role in reducing emissions from hard-to-abate sectors.

Reforestation and afforestation are natural mitigation strategies that enhance carbon sequestration. Trees absorb carbon dioxide from the atmosphere and store it in their biomass, making forests vital carbon sinks. By restoring degraded lands and planting new forests, we can increase the Earth's capacity to absorb carbon and mitigate climate change. Protecting existing forests is equally important, as deforestation releases stored carbon and reduces the planet's ability to sequester future emissions.

Adaptation strategies, on the other hand, focus on adjusting to the impacts of climate change that are already occurring or anticipated. These strategies are essential for building resilience and reducing vulnerability to climate-related risks. One of the key areas of adaptation is infrastructure development. By designing and constructing resilient infrastructure, such as flood defenses, stormwater management systems, and climate-resilient buildings, communities can better withstand extreme weather events and rising sea levels.

Water resource management is another critical aspect of adaptation. Climate change is expected to alter precipitation patterns and increase the frequency and severity of droughts and floods. By implementing integrated water management practices, such as rainwater harvesting, efficient irrigation systems, and wastewater recycling, communities can ensure a reliable water supply and reduce the risk of water-related disasters.

Agriculture is particularly vulnerable to the impacts of climate change, with shifts in temperature and precipitation affecting crop yields and food security. Adaptation strategies in agriculture include the development of climate-resilient crops, improved soil management practices, and the adoption of sustainable farming techniques. By diversifying crops and implementing agroforestry systems, farmers can enhance their resilience to climate variability and reduce their reliance on chemical inputs.

Ecosystem-based adaptation approaches leverage the natural resilience of ecosystems to buffer against climate impacts. By protecting and restoring natural habitats, such as wetlands, mangroves, and coral reefs, we can enhance their ability to provide essential services, such as flood protection, water purification, and carbon sequestration. These approaches not only support biodiversity but also offer cost-effective solutions for climate adaptation.

Community involvement and stakeholder engagement are crucial for the success of both mitigation and adaptation efforts. Local communities often have valuable knowledge and a vested interest in the sustainable management of natural resources. By involving communities in decision-making processes and providing them with the tools and resources needed to participate in climate action, we can build trust and foster a sense of ownership and responsibility.

Policy frameworks and regulatory measures play a vital role in supporting mitigation and adaptation strategies. Governments can implement policies that promote sustainable practices, such as setting emission reduction targets, enforcing environmental standards, and providing incentives for renewable energy and energy efficiency. International agreements, such as the Paris Agreement, provide a framework for countries to work together to address climate change and promote sustainable development.

Education and awareness are key components of efforts to mitigate and adapt to climate change. By raising awareness of the impacts of climate change and the importance of taking action, individuals and communities can make informed choices that support sustainability. Educational programs, public awareness campaigns, and community initiatives can empower people to take action and advocate for change.

The Role of Policy and International Agreements

Policies and international agreements are pivotal in shaping the global response to climate change, providing frameworks for cooperation, setting targets, and guiding national and international efforts. These instruments are essential for coordinating actions across borders, ensuring accountability, and mobilizing resources to address the multifaceted challenges posed by a changing climate.

The foundation of climate policy lies in understanding the science of climate change and translating it into actionable strategies. Governments, informed by scientific research and data, develop policies that aim to reduce greenhouse gas emissions, promote sustainable development, and enhance resilience to climate impacts. These policies can take various forms, including regulations, incentives, and market-based mechanisms, each tailored to the specific needs and circumstances of a country or region.

Regulatory measures are a common approach to climate policy, setting standards and limits on emissions from various sectors. These regulations can include emission caps for industries, fuel efficiency standards for vehicles, and building codes that promote energy efficiency. By establishing clear rules and guidelines, governments can drive innovation and encourage the adoption of cleaner technologies and practices.

Incentives and subsidies are another tool used to promote sustainable practices and reduce emissions. By providing financial support for renewable energy projects, energy efficiency improvements, and sustainable agriculture, governments can lower the barriers to entry for these technologies and encourage their widespread adoption. Tax credits, grants, and low-interest loans are examples of incentives that can stimulate investment in green technologies and infrastructure.

Market-based mechanisms, such as carbon pricing and cap-and-trade systems, offer flexible and cost-effective ways to reduce emissions. Carbon pricing assigns a monetary value to carbon emissions, encouraging businesses and individuals to reduce their carbon footprint. Cap-and-trade systems set a limit on emissions and allow companies to buy and sell emission allowances, creating a financial incentive to reduce emissions. These mechanisms harness the power of the market to drive emission reductions and promote innovation.

International agreements play a crucial role in coordinating global efforts to address climate change. The United Nations Framework Convention on Climate Change (UNFCCC) serves as the primary international platform for climate negotiations, bringing together countries to discuss and implement strategies for mitigating and adapting to climate change. The UNFCCC provides a framework for cooperation, facilitating the exchange of information, technology, and resources among countries.

The Kyoto Protocol, adopted in 1997, was one of the first major international agreements to set binding emission reduction targets for developed countries. While it marked a significant step forward in international climate policy, its limitations, such as the exclusion of developing countries and the withdrawal of key participants, highlighted the need for a more inclusive and flexible approach.

The Paris Agreement, adopted in 2015, represents a landmark achievement in international climate diplomacy. Unlike the Kyoto Protocol, the Paris Agreement includes commitments from both developed and developing countries, recognizing the shared responsibility of all nations to address climate change. The agreement aims to limit global warming to well below 2 degrees Celsius above pre-industrial levels, with efforts to limit the temperature increase to 1.5 degrees Celsius.

A key feature of the Paris Agreement is its emphasis on nationally determined contributions (NDCs), which allow countries to set their own emission reduction targets based on their unique circumstances and capabilities. This bottom-up approach encourages countries to take ownership of their climate commitments and fosters a sense of collective responsibility. The agreement also includes mechanisms for transparency and accountability, ensuring that countries report on their progress and update their NDCs regularly.

Financial support and technology transfer are critical components of international climate agreements, enabling developing countries to implement mitigation and adaptation measures. The Green Climate Fund, established under the UNFCCC, provides financial assistance to developing countries for climate-related projects and initiatives. By mobilizing resources and facilitating access to technology, international agreements can help bridge the gap between developed and developing countries and promote equitable climate action.

The role of non-state actors, such as businesses, cities, and civil society organizations, is increasingly recognized in international climate policy. These actors can complement government efforts by driving innovation, raising awareness, and implementing local solutions. Initiatives like the Global Covenant of Mayors for Climate & Energy and the We Mean Business coalition demonstrate the potential for collaboration between public and private sectors in advancing climate goals.

Despite the progress made through international agreements, challenges remain in achieving global climate targets. Political, economic, and social factors can influence the willingness and ability of countries to fulfill their commitments. Ensuring compliance and accountability is a complex task, requiring robust monitoring and reporting mechanisms. Additionally, the need for greater ambition and urgency in addressing climate change is evident, as current commitments fall short of the targets set by the Paris Agreement.

Public awareness and engagement are essential for the success of climate policies and international agreements. By raising awareness of the impacts of climate change and the importance of taking action, individuals and communities can support and advocate for effective climate policies. Educational programs, public awareness campaigns, and community initiatives can empower people to participate in climate action and hold governments accountable for their commitments.

Chapter 5

Innovative Solutions for Sustainable Living

Renewable Energy Technologies

Harnessing the power of renewable energy technologies is a cornerstone in the quest for a sustainable future. These technologies offer a viable alternative to fossil fuels, reducing greenhouse gas emissions and mitigating the impacts of climate change. As the world grapples with the urgent need to transition to cleaner energy sources, understanding the potential and challenges of renewable energy technologies becomes increasingly important.

Solar energy, one of the most abundant and accessible forms of renewable energy, has seen remarkable advancements in recent years. Photovoltaic (PV) cells, which convert sunlight directly into electricity, have become more efficient and affordable, making solar power a competitive option for both residential and commercial use. The scalability of solar technology allows it to be deployed in a variety of settings, from small rooftop installations to large solar farms. Innovations such as solar panels integrated into building materials and solar tracking systems that follow the sun's path further enhance the efficiency and versatility of solar energy.

Wind energy, harnessed through wind turbines, is another key player in the renewable energy landscape. Wind farms, both onshore and offshore, have the capacity to generate significant amounts of electricity with minimal environmental impact. Advances in turbine design, including larger rotor diameters and taller towers, have increased the efficiency and output of wind energy systems. Offshore wind farms, in particular, benefit from stronger and more consistent winds, offering the potential for substantial energy generation. However, challenges such as the environmental impact on marine ecosystems and the need for robust infrastructure must be addressed to fully realize the potential of offshore wind energy.

Hydropower, the largest source of renewable electricity worldwide, utilizes the energy of flowing water to generate power. Traditional hydropower plants, which rely on dams and reservoirs, provide a reliable and consistent source of energy. However, they can have significant ecological and social impacts, including habitat disruption and displacement of communities. To mitigate these effects, run-of-the-river and small-scale hydropower systems offer more sustainable alternatives, generating electricity with minimal environmental disturbance. These systems harness the natural flow of rivers without the need for large reservoirs, making them suitable for a wider range of locations.

Biomass energy, derived from organic materials such as plant matter and animal waste, offers a renewable alternative to fossil fuels for heating, electricity, and transportation. Biomass can be converted into biofuels, such as ethanol and biodiesel, which can be used in existing engines and infrastructure. The use of agricultural residues, forestry by-products, and dedicated energy crops for biomass production can reduce waste and promote sustainable land management. However, the sustainability of biomass energy depends on responsible sourcing and management practices to avoid negative impacts on food security and biodiversity.

Geothermal energy, which taps into the Earth's internal heat, provides a reliable and consistent source of power. Geothermal power plants, typically located in regions with high volcanic activity, use steam or hot water from underground reservoirs to drive turbines and generate electricity. In addition to electricity generation, geothermal energy can be used for direct heating applications, such as district heating systems and greenhouse agriculture. The potential for geothermal energy is vast, but its development is limited by geographical constraints and the need for significant upfront investment.

The integration of renewable energy technologies into existing energy systems presents both opportunities and challenges. The intermittent nature of solar and wind energy requires the development of energy storage solutions and grid management strategies to ensure a stable and reliable power supply. Battery storage systems, such as lithium-ion and flow batteries, are essential for storing excess energy generated during peak production periods and releasing it when demand is high. Additionally, smart grid technologies, which use digital communication and automation to optimize energy distribution, play a crucial role in managing the variability of renewable energy sources.

Policy support and financial incentives are critical for the widespread adoption of renewable energy technologies. Governments can implement policies that promote research and development, provide subsidies and tax credits, and set renewable energy targets. These measures can lower the cost of renewable energy projects and encourage investment in clean energy infrastructure. International cooperation and knowledge sharing are also essential for accelerating the deployment of renewable energy technologies and addressing global energy challenges.

Public awareness and engagement are vital for the success of renewable energy initiatives. By raising awareness of the benefits and potential of renewable energy technologies, individuals and communities can support and advocate for clean energy solutions. Educational programs, public awareness campaigns, and community-based projects can empower people to participate in the transition to renewable energy and make informed choices about their energy consumption.

Sustainable Agriculture Practices

Sustainable agriculture practices are essential for ensuring food security, preserving natural resources, and mitigating the impacts of climate change. As the global population continues to grow, the demand for food increases, placing immense pressure on agricultural systems. Traditional farming methods, often reliant on chemical inputs and monocultures, can lead to soil degradation, water pollution, and biodiversity loss. In contrast, sustainable agriculture seeks to balance productivity with environmental stewardship, promoting practices that enhance ecosystem health and resilience.

One of the fundamental principles of sustainable agriculture is soil health. Healthy soil is the foundation of productive farming, supporting plant growth, water retention, and nutrient cycling. Practices such as crop rotation, cover cropping, and reduced tillage help maintain and improve soil structure and fertility. Crop rotation involves alternating different crops in a sequence, which can disrupt pest and disease cycles and improve soil nutrient balance. Cover crops, such as legumes and grasses, are planted during fallow periods to protect the soil from erosion, suppress weeds, and fix atmospheric nitrogen. Reduced tillage minimizes soil disturbance, preserving soil organic matter and reducing erosion.

Agroecology, an approach that applies ecological principles to agricultural systems, emphasizes the importance of biodiversity and ecosystem services. By fostering diverse plant and animal communities, agroecology enhances resilience to pests, diseases, and climate variability. Intercropping, the practice of growing multiple crops in proximity, can increase biodiversity and improve resource use efficiency. For example, planting legumes alongside cereals can enhance nitrogen availability and reduce the need for synthetic fertilizers. Agroforestry, which integrates trees and shrubs into agricultural landscapes, provides additional benefits such as carbon sequestration, habitat for wildlife, and protection from wind and water erosion.

Water management is a critical aspect of sustainable agriculture, particularly in regions prone to drought or water scarcity. Efficient irrigation systems, such as drip or sprinkler irrigation, deliver water directly to the plant roots, reducing evaporation and runoff. Rainwater harvesting and water recycling can supplement irrigation and reduce reliance on external water sources. Additionally, practices such as contour farming and terracing can help conserve water and prevent soil erosion on sloped lands.

Integrated pest management (IPM) is a sustainable approach to controlling pests and diseases, minimizing the use of chemical pesticides. IPM combines biological, cultural, and mechanical control methods to manage pest populations and reduce crop damage. Biological control involves the use of natural predators or parasites to suppress pest populations, while cultural practices, such as crop rotation and sanitation, can disrupt pest life cycles. Mechanical controls, such as traps and barriers, provide physical protection against pests. By reducing reliance on chemical inputs, IPM promotes biodiversity and reduces the risk of pesticide resistance and environmental contamination.

Sustainable livestock management practices focus on animal welfare, resource efficiency, and environmental impact. Rotational grazing, where livestock are moved between pastures, allows vegetation to recover and reduces soil compaction and erosion. This practice can enhance pasture productivity and biodiversity while improving soil health. Integrating livestock with crop production can also create synergies, as manure provides a valuable source of organic fertilizer, and crop residues can serve as animal feed. By optimizing resource use and minimizing waste, sustainable livestock systems contribute to a more circular and resilient agricultural system.

Organic farming, a subset of sustainable agriculture, prohibits the use of synthetic fertilizers and pesticides, relying instead on natural inputs and processes. Organic practices emphasize soil health, biodiversity, and ecological balance, often incorporating techniques such as composting, green manures, and biological pest control. While organic farming can offer environmental benefits, it may require more land and labor to achieve comparable yields to conventional systems. Therefore, a combination of organic and other sustainable practices may be necessary to meet global food demands while minimizing environmental impact.

Community-supported agriculture (CSA) and local food systems promote sustainability by connecting consumers directly with producers. CSA programs allow consumers to purchase shares of a farm's harvest, providing farmers with a stable income and reducing the need for intermediaries. Local food systems shorten supply chains, reducing transportation emissions and supporting regional economies. By fostering a closer relationship between producers and consumers, these systems encourage transparency, trust, and a greater appreciation for the value of sustainable agriculture.

Education and knowledge sharing are vital for the adoption and success of sustainable agriculture practices. Farmers, extension agents, and researchers must collaborate to develop and disseminate best practices, technologies, and innovations. Farmer field schools, workshops, and demonstration plots provide opportunities for hands-on learning and peer-to-peer exchange. By building local capacity and empowering farmers with the knowledge and skills needed to implement sustainable practices, communities can enhance their resilience and food security.

Policy support and incentives play a crucial role in promoting sustainable agriculture. Governments can implement policies that encourage the adoption of sustainable practices, such as providing financial assistance for conservation programs, supporting research and development, and setting environmental standards. International cooperation and knowledge sharing can also facilitate the transfer of sustainable technologies and practices across borders, helping to address global challenges such as climate change and food security.

Green Urban Planning and Architecture

Green urban planning and architecture represent a transformative approach to designing cities that prioritize sustainability, resilience, and the well-being of their inhabitants. As urban populations continue to swell, the need for innovative solutions to address environmental challenges and improve quality of life becomes increasingly urgent. By integrating green principles into urban development, cities can reduce their ecological footprint, enhance biodiversity, and create vibrant, livable spaces for all.

Central to green urban planning is the concept of sustainable land use. This involves optimizing the use of available land to accommodate growth while preserving natural ecosystems and minimizing sprawl. Mixed-use development, which combines residential, commercial, and recreational spaces, promotes efficient land use and reduces the need for long commutes. By creating walkable neighborhoods with access to public transportation, cities can decrease reliance on cars, lower emissions, and improve air quality.

Green spaces, such as parks, gardens, and urban forests, play a crucial role in enhancing urban environments. These areas provide essential ecosystem services, including air purification, temperature regulation, and stormwater management. They also offer recreational opportunities and improve mental health by providing residents with access to nature. Incorporating green spaces into urban design can enhance biodiversity, support pollinators, and create wildlife corridors that connect fragmented habitats.

Water management is a critical component of green urban planning, particularly in the face of climate change and increasing urbanization. Sustainable urban drainage systems (SUDS) use natural processes to manage stormwater, reducing the risk of flooding and improving water quality. Techniques such as permeable pavements, green roofs, and rain gardens allow rainwater to infiltrate the ground, replenishing aquifers and reducing runoff. By integrating these systems into urban design, cities can enhance resilience to extreme weather events and promote sustainable water use.

Energy efficiency is a cornerstone of green architecture, with buildings accounting for a significant portion of global energy consumption and emissions. Designing energy-efficient buildings involves optimizing insulation, ventilation, and lighting to reduce energy use and enhance comfort. Passive solar design, which maximizes natural light and heat, can significantly reduce the need for artificial lighting and heating. Additionally, incorporating renewable energy sources, such as solar panels and wind turbines, into building design can further reduce emissions and promote energy independence.

The use of sustainable materials is another key aspect of green architecture. By selecting materials with low environmental impact, such as recycled, locally sourced, or rapidly renewable resources, architects can reduce the carbon footprint of construction projects. Innovative materials, such as cross-laminated timber and rammed earth, offer sustainable alternatives to traditional building materials like concrete and steel. These materials not only reduce emissions but also enhance the aesthetic and thermal properties of buildings.

Adaptive reuse and retrofitting of existing structures offer opportunities to enhance sustainability without the need for new construction. By repurposing old buildings and upgrading their energy systems, cities can preserve cultural heritage, reduce waste, and minimize the environmental impact of development. Retrofitting can include measures such as improving insulation, installing energy-efficient windows, and upgrading heating and cooling systems. These interventions can significantly reduce energy consumption and extend the lifespan of buildings.

Transportation planning is integral to green urban development, with a focus on reducing emissions and promoting sustainable mobility. Public transportation systems, such as buses, trains, and trams, offer efficient and low-emission alternatives to private vehicles. Expanding and improving public transit networks can reduce congestion, improve air quality, and enhance accessibility for all residents. Additionally, promoting active transportation, such as walking and cycling, through the development of pedestrian-friendly infrastructure and bike lanes, can further reduce emissions and improve public health.

Community engagement and participation are essential for the success of green urban planning initiatives. By involving residents in the planning process, cities can ensure that development projects meet the needs and priorities of the community. Participatory planning processes, such as workshops, surveys, and public consultations, provide opportunities for residents to contribute their ideas and feedback. This collaborative approach fosters a sense of ownership and responsibility, encouraging residents to support and maintain green initiatives.

Policy frameworks and incentives play a crucial role in promoting green urban planning and architecture. Governments can implement policies that set sustainability standards, provide financial incentives for green building projects, and support research and innovation. Zoning regulations and building codes can be updated to encourage sustainable practices, such as the incorporation of green roofs, energy-efficient design, and mixed-use development. By creating an enabling environment for green development, policymakers can drive the transition to sustainable cities.

Education and awareness are vital for fostering a culture of sustainability in urban environments. By raising awareness of the benefits of green urban planning and architecture, individuals and communities can make informed choices and advocate for sustainable development. Educational programs, public awareness campaigns, and community initiatives can empower residents to participate in green initiatives and adopt sustainable practices in their daily lives.

Waste Reduction and Recycling Innovations

Waste reduction and recycling innovations are pivotal in addressing the mounting environmental challenges posed by increasing waste generation. As global consumption rises, so does the volume of waste, straining landfills, polluting ecosystems, and contributing to greenhouse gas emissions. Embracing innovative strategies for waste reduction and recycling not only conserves resources but also fosters a circular economy, where materials are reused and repurposed, minimizing the need for virgin resources.

At the heart of waste reduction is the principle of minimizing waste at its source. This involves rethinking product design, packaging, and consumption patterns to prevent waste before it occurs. Companies are increasingly adopting eco-design principles, creating products that are durable, repairable, and recyclable. By using fewer materials and designing for disassembly, manufacturers can reduce waste and facilitate recycling. Consumers, too, play a crucial role by choosing products with minimal packaging, opting for reusable items, and supporting brands committed to sustainability.

The concept of zero waste, which aims to eliminate waste through responsible production, consumption, and recovery, is gaining traction worldwide. Communities and businesses adopting zero waste practices focus on reducing, reusing, and recycling materials to divert waste from landfills and incinerators. This holistic approach encourages collaboration among stakeholders, including governments, businesses, and citizens, to create systems that support waste reduction and resource recovery.

Recycling innovations are transforming the way materials are recovered and repurposed. Advanced sorting technologies, such as optical sorters and robotic systems, enhance the efficiency and accuracy of recycling facilities. These technologies can identify and separate materials based on their composition, color, and shape, improving the quality of recycled materials and reducing contamination. Additionally, chemical recycling processes, which break down plastics into their molecular components, offer the potential to recycle materials that are difficult to process through traditional mechanical methods.

The rise of the sharing economy is another innovative approach to waste reduction. By facilitating the sharing and reuse of goods and services, platforms like car-sharing, tool libraries, and clothing rental services reduce the demand for new products and extend the lifespan of existing ones. This shift from ownership to access not only conserves resources but also fosters community connections and reduces environmental impact.

Composting, a natural process that transforms organic waste into nutrient-rich soil, is an effective way to reduce waste and enhance soil health. By diverting food scraps and yard waste from landfills, composting reduces methane emissions and returns valuable nutrients to the soil. Community composting programs, which provide residents with access to composting facilities and education, can significantly increase participation and awareness. Innovations in composting technology, such as in-vessel systems and anaerobic digesters, offer scalable solutions for urban and industrial settings.

E-waste, or electronic waste, poses a unique challenge due to its complex composition and potential environmental hazards. Innovations in e-waste recycling focus on recovering valuable materials, such as precious metals and rare earth elements, while safely managing hazardous components. Extended producer responsibility (EPR) programs, which hold manufacturers accountable for the end-of-life management of their products, incentivize the design of more sustainable electronics and support the development of efficient recycling systems.

Education and awareness are critical components of successful waste reduction and recycling initiatives. By raising awareness of the environmental impact of waste and the benefits of recycling, individuals and communities can make informed choices and adopt sustainable practices. Educational programs, public awareness campaigns, and community workshops can empower people to participate in waste reduction efforts and advocate for systemic change.

Policy frameworks and incentives play a vital role in promoting waste reduction and recycling innovations. Governments can implement policies that set waste reduction targets, provide financial support for recycling infrastructure, and encourage the development of sustainable products. Regulations, such as bans on single-use plastics and landfill taxes, can drive behavior change and support the transition to a circular economy. International cooperation and knowledge sharing can also facilitate the exchange of best practices and technologies, helping to address global waste challenges.

Collaboration among stakeholders, including governments, businesses, and civil society, is essential for advancing waste reduction and recycling innovations. By working together, stakeholders can develop integrated solutions that address the root causes of waste and promote resource efficiency. Public-private partnerships, industry collaborations, and community initiatives can leverage resources and expertise to drive innovation and create scalable solutions.

The Role of Technology in Ecological Conservation

Technology has emerged as a powerful ally in the quest for ecological conservation, offering innovative tools and solutions to protect and restore the natural world. As human activities continue to exert pressure on ecosystems, the integration of technology into conservation efforts becomes increasingly vital. From monitoring wildlife populations to combating illegal activities, technology provides the means to enhance our understanding of ecosystems and implement effective conservation strategies.

One of the most significant contributions of technology to conservation is the ability to monitor and collect data on wildlife and their habitats. Remote sensing technologies, such as satellite imagery and aerial drones, allow conservationists to observe large and inaccessible areas with unprecedented detail. These tools provide valuable insights into land use changes, deforestation, and habitat fragmentation, enabling timely interventions to protect critical ecosystems. Drones, equipped with high-resolution cameras and sensors, can capture detailed images and data, offering a bird's-eye view of landscapes and wildlife populations.

Wildlife tracking technologies, such as GPS collars and radio telemetry, have revolutionized the study of animal behavior and movement patterns. By attaching tracking devices to animals, researchers can gather data on migration routes, habitat use, and social interactions. This information is crucial for identifying critical habitats, understanding species' ecological needs, and developing targeted conservation plans. For example, tracking data can inform the creation of wildlife corridors that connect fragmented habitats, allowing animals to move freely and maintain genetic diversity.

Acoustic monitoring is another innovative approach to studying wildlife, particularly in remote or dense environments. By deploying audio recording devices in the field, researchers can capture the sounds of animals, such as birds, bats, and marine mammals. Analyzing these recordings provides insights into species presence, abundance, and behavior, as well as the impacts of environmental changes on acoustic communities. Acoustic monitoring is especially valuable for studying elusive or nocturnal species that are difficult to observe visually.

Technology also plays a crucial role in combating illegal activities that threaten biodiversity, such as poaching and illegal logging. Advanced surveillance systems, including camera traps and motion sensors, can detect and record human activity in protected areas, providing real-time alerts to rangers and law enforcement. These systems enhance the ability to monitor vast and remote areas, increasing the chances of intercepting illegal activities before they cause significant harm. Additionally, satellite imagery and data analytics can be used to identify and track illegal logging operations, enabling authorities to take swift action.

Conservation technology extends to the restoration of degraded ecosystems, offering innovative solutions for habitat rehabilitation. Techniques such as drone-assisted reforestation and precision agriculture enable the efficient planting and monitoring of vegetation in areas affected by deforestation or land degradation. Drones can disperse seeds over large areas, reaching inaccessible or hazardous locations, while precision agriculture technologies optimize resource use and improve the success of restoration efforts. These approaches accelerate the recovery of ecosystems, enhancing biodiversity and ecosystem services.

Citizen science, facilitated by technology, empowers individuals and communities to contribute to conservation efforts. Mobile apps and online platforms enable people to collect and share data on local wildlife, habitats, and environmental conditions. This crowdsourced information complements scientific research, providing valuable data for monitoring biodiversity and informing conservation decisions. Citizen science initiatives also raise awareness and foster a sense of stewardship, encouraging people to take an active role in protecting their natural surroundings.

Genetic technologies, such as DNA barcoding and environmental DNA (eDNA) analysis, offer powerful tools for biodiversity assessment and monitoring. DNA barcoding involves sequencing a short genetic marker from an organism to identify its species, while eDNA analysis detects genetic material shed by organisms into the environment. These techniques enable the rapid and accurate identification of species, even from small or degraded samples. They are particularly useful for monitoring aquatic ecosystems, where traditional survey methods may be challenging or invasive.

The integration of artificial intelligence (AI) and machine learning into conservation efforts enhances the ability to analyze complex data sets and make informed decisions. AI algorithms can process vast amounts of data from various sources, such as satellite imagery, acoustic recordings, and camera trap photos, to identify patterns and trends. Machine learning models can predict species distributions, assess habitat suitability, and evaluate the impacts of environmental changes. These insights support the development of adaptive management strategies that respond to dynamic ecological conditions.

Despite the potential of technology to advance conservation, challenges remain in its implementation and accessibility. The cost of acquiring and maintaining advanced technologies can be prohibitive, particularly for conservation organizations with limited resources. Additionally, the effective use of technology requires technical expertise and training, which may not be readily available in all regions. To address these challenges, partnerships between governments, NGOs, and the private sector are essential to provide funding, training, and support for technology-driven conservation initiatives.

Ethical considerations also arise in the use of technology for conservation, particularly regarding privacy and data security. The deployment of surveillance technologies in protected areas must balance the need for monitoring with respect for the rights and privacy of local communities. Transparent and inclusive decision-making processes, involving stakeholders and indigenous peoples, are crucial to ensure that conservation technologies are used responsibly and equitably.

www.ingramcontent.com/pod-product-compliance
Lightning Source LLC
Chambersburg PA
CBHW072025150726
47999CB00002B/763